T0277279

Praise for *Unlock*

"Turning around a stalled company is one of the hardest tasks in business. But Matt Hulett knows how to do it—and now he's here to teach the rest of us. This book will help any leader shed entrenched thinking and bring fresh insight to their work."

DANIEL H. PINK, #1 *New York Times*–bestselling author of *When, Drive,* and *To Sell Is Human*

"There's nobody better than Matt Hulett to teach business leaders how to turn around a company. His framework is an insightful and efficient way to determine the potential of a business and then move it from stagnation to success. He's done this himself, multiple times. *Unlock* is an invaluable guide for any leader. I've been fortunate to know Matt for years, and I've benefited from his teaching and experience. His track record of turning around companies is unparalleled, so it's no surprise that his book contains so much valuable information. This exceptional and efficient book should be on the desk or e-reader of every executive."

SPENCER RASCOFF, co-founder, Zillow, Pacaso, dot.LA, and Hotwire

"From early-stage startups to large public companies, and consumer businesses to B2B enterprises, Matt Hulett presents a prolific guide full of helpful information to assess and position your company for success. This book takes you through every imaginable scenario, along with extensive Q&As, so you can apply all of the insights to your own situation. Read this book—and learn from one of the best!"

CAROLINE TSAY, CEO and co-founder, Compute Software; board member, The Coca-Cola Company and Morningstar

"I've served on Matt Hulett's board, competed with him, and count him as a highly trusted consigliere. He is thoughtful, and the wisdom he used to impart only to a small circle is now available to everyone. Read this book and you will be armed with the wisdom and tools to turn around any company."

ROB SOLOMON, chairman, GoFundMe; seasoned Silicon Valley executive

"Matt Hulett is recognized in the technology ecosystem as a proven turnaround leader. His many experiences give him unique insight which he graciously shares in this book. *Unlock* is a playbook anyone can use."

LO TONEY, founder/managing partner, Plexo Capital; former partner, GV (Google Ventures)

"Matt Hulett's book condenses his thirty years of key learnings and practical insights from the world of tech. *Unlock* is useful for entrepreneurs starting their first company as well as for those who are growing a successful company."

RICCARDO ZACCONI, co-founder, King (developer of *Candy Crush*)

"*Unlock* isn't just about thinking outside of the box—it is about breaking out of the box. Cerebral and practical, *Unlock* will shake up your approach and focus your efforts on true value creation. This book combines great theory with useful examples that you can apply to your own business challenges."

LAURENCE FRANKLIN, former CEO, Coach and TUMI

UNLOCK

5 Questions to Unleash Your Company's Hidden Power

UNLOCK

MATT HULETT

FORMER PRESIDENT OF
ROSETTA STONE AND **EXPEDIA**

PAGE TWO

Cataloguing in publication information is
available from Library and Archives Canada.
ISBN 978-1-77458-154-4 (hardcover)
ISBN 978-1-77458-155-1 (ebook)
ISBN 978-1-77458-250-3 (audiobook)

Page Two
pagetwo.com

Edited by Scott Steedman
Copyedited by Christine Lyseng Savage
Proofread by Alison Strobel
Jacket design by Jennifer Lum with Peter Cocking
Interior design and illustrations by Setareh Ashrafologhalai
Indexed by Donald Howes
Printed and bound in Canada by Friesens
Distributed in Canada by Raincoast Books
Distributed in the US and internationally by Macmillan

22 23 24 25 26   5 4 3 2 1

startupwhisperer.com

To my mom.

*For always being there for me. For always giving
me encouragement. For teaching me the
value of grit and creativity. And, when I needed it,
for giving me a kick in the ass.*

CONTENTS

INTRODUCTION

REMEMBER THE 2008 action movie *Taken*? It stars the gruff Irish tough guy Liam Neeson, whose seventeen-year-old daughter has been kidnapped by a band of Albanian smugglers. OK, it wasn't a classic. But there's one very famous scene, when Neeson's character threatens the lead kidnapper in a manner that etched its words into my brain. How can we forget these lines: "I don't know who you are. I don't know what you want. If you are looking for ransom, I can tell you I don't have money... but what I *do* have [is] a very particular set of skills. Skills I have acquired over a very long career. Skills that make me a nightmare for people like you."

When I think back on my career, I hear those words in my head. Probably because I have taken on jobs and companies that most operators would have avoided. Messy jobs: the turnarounds, the pivots, jobs where you have to go in and make an impact. Fast. So I do feel like a man with a particular set of skills—skills that most of my peers don't have.

I'm always brought into situations where something is broken and needs to be fixed. Maybe the company is in the wrong business overall, or the strategy is bad—or really, maybe everything is just bad. Not enough capital, or the CEO and founder is the wrong fit. Whatever it is, something's wrong, and I'm brought in to fix it.

I'm not sure why that is. I have no desire to seek therapy or pursue my Jungian archetypes. Maybe I did something in a previous life that set me on this path. Maybe I'm paying for some forgotten sin. I'd rather believe that I'm drawn to messy situations because of my upbringing. I was brought up in a divorced family and was made the man of the house at a very young age. Getting a lot of responsibility all at once thrusts you into triage mode, meaning you're always looking at the opportunity, assessing the situation, designing a plan of action, and then executing it. In the military experience it's called an OODA loop: Observe, Orient, Decide, and Act. I have built my own version of the OODA loop to unlock value in companies, or at least to determine if there *is* value to be unlocked.

I have worked in public and private technology companies for the last thirty years. I have worked in so many different industries and with so many different business models that I have built a knack for pattern recognition. I feel the need to discuss how my career has ping-ponged from many different types of companies because I think it can help others who are striving for success. I have experience growing businesses from zero to a billion dollars in gross sales, multiple wins transforming poor-performing companies to double-digit growth—and I have screwed up along the way too. I will be open about those wins and losses. This book was written with a lifetime of blood, sweat, and tears that business leaders can learn from.

When I started taking over companies as the CEO or president, there was no instruction manual I could read to show me how to fix or transform them. Most of the books I could get my hands on talked about "optimizing for value." This was code for cutting costs. If you read between the lines, cutting operating expenses was pretty much the only strategy they recommended. I could never figure out why there were not more books written about how to change your market position.

You *can* change your market position. You can pivot, turn around, and/or refocus your growth business. You can change your course. You can change your destiny. The business world is not Greek theater—nothing is predestined. I truly believe that you can drive a new destiny for your business and for your career.

There are many famous examples, some quite recent. For example, a game company called Slack pivoted to the chat and messaging product we all know and love today. There are many other examples of early-stage companies pivoting their focus. But can an existing business reimagine itself? Absolutely. Think about Apple and its amazing transformations after Steve Jobs's return in 1996: a stream of product advancements, starting with the iMac, the iPod, the iPhone, and so many more.

Can You Turn a Dog Into a Star? Yes!

The Boston Consulting Group has a well-known two-by-two (2×2) growth matrix that has been at the forefront of my career. Each box on the matrix determines the appropriate capital allocation strategy. I didn't even know that it was possible to change a business from one square in the matrix to another until I got call after call asking me to do just that. These calls typically start out with, "Hi, Matt. I have an asset with a little bit of hair on it. Growth has slowed. The team isn't innovating and hasn't really figured out what to do. The competition is starting to heat up, and we investors are getting anxious. Interested?" In BCG terms, I called this, "Will you turn my dog into a star?"

Can You Turn a Dog Into a Star?

BOSTON CONSULTING GROUP, GROWTH SHARE MATRIX, 1968

Let me explain, with reference to the diagram. Typically, neither a dog nor a cash cow is growing. A question mark doesn't have high market share, but it's growing fast. Alas, everyone wants to be a star. And to be clear, not every business can be turned around. Some are very good lifestyle businesses, but they're never going to become stars. And some businesses are just too antiquated—turning them around would require too much capital.

So how can you turn your business into a high-market-share, high-growth company? I felt compelled to write this book to try and answer that question, and because I couldn't find any resources for myself. The other primary motivator is to provide an inexpensive resource to give back to the entrepreneur and business community in a way that encourages us to include more diversity. Creating lower barriers for a broader array of business and product thinkers to thrive is just a net good thing for the planet.

My Unique Journey

Before I lay out my philosophy on unlocking value, I'd like to first give you a sense of the diversity of businesses I have been involved with in my career. I haven't stuck with one vertical or business model over my thirty-plus years. While perhaps not the smartest thing to do from a career perspective, this has certainly given me an outlook that ranges from consumer to enterprise, from freemium to SaaS (software as a service) to DTC (direct to consumer). I have seen a lot.

I started my technology career in 1990. I was a sophomore in college with no tech background. I had paid for a lot of my school and was desperate to get a job. I found a paid internship at a reinsurance brokerage, performing junior-level database programming. I didn't know how to program and might have fudged a little bit on my technical prowess. This was soon obvious to everyone around me, including my supervisor, so my internship dried up fast. I was scrambling to make ends meet, so I decided to work for a temp agency. After a lot of clerical work, I received an assignment at a software company, shrink-wrapping boxes. Yes, we used to do that back in the days when your computer program was stored on a floppy disk.

I was very interested in business and was attending the undergraduate business school at the University of Washington. I remember listening to a product manager for Procter & Gamble speak at a campus event. I was fascinated by his description of the product manager as the "product champion" at a company. Fortunately for me, my job at the software company turned into an internship in product management. I stayed with this company, WRQ, after college, learning about networking technology, the underpinning of the Internet.

A kid named Marc Andreessen had just launched a free web browser called NCSA Mosaic (which became Netscape).

I was intrigued with connecting tools like this with computers and services all around the world. I found a company in Seattle called Progressive Networks, a pioneer in streaming audio and video, and I landed a job as the first product manager for a product called RealPlayer. It soon became one of the most popular products on the Internet.

My time at Progressive Networks was amazing and challenging. The culture was fast-paced and hard-charging. And moving from a niche software company to a company that was building the next mass medium over the Internet was a game changer. The change in scale was insane, especially for a young product manager. When I started, RealPlayer was being downloaded something like 300 times a day; three years later, we were up to 300,000 times a day. It was a never-ending joyride, and I still look back at those days with fondness.

I started to get the itch to do something else. Progressive Networks, renamed RealNetworks, had gone public and was getting big. I worked with a talented business development executive named Mika Salmi, who envisioned content being streamed across your phone, your PC, your Internet-connected TV, etc. This was very prescient at the time, considering most of us were browsing the Internet over dial-up modems. He also wanted to own the intellectual property (IP), so he started to license student films, which were bite-sized and suitable for Internet consumption (remember, this was before YouTube). The idea was to create an Internet-based entertainment company that owned a large catalog of live-action and animated short-form content. The company was AtomFilms, and I became its president. We had a who's who of investors and board members. It was backed by Sequoia Capital, Intel, Allen & Company, and many others.

My new role as president of a startup was quite a change from being a group product manager. We were hot—long on vision but short on cash flow. Then the dot-com bubble burst (kids, ask your parents), and we combined our business with a spinoff of Macromedia (which later became Adobe) called Shockwave. The Web 1.0 period, a very strange time, suddenly ended. Our advertisers, our main source of revenue, disappeared overnight. We had huge contracts with celebrities to provide us with content—Tim Burton, the *South Park* creators, etc.—and we were too big to support our shrinking revenues. The whole city of San Francisco shut its doors with the demise of the tech industry. I was used to being just a product guy, not having to worry about an entire company. But as president of a floundering startup, I was now on the hook.

For the first time I had to manage a P&L (profit and loss). We had major losses and had to cut costs if we were going to survive. I had to lay off a lot of people. This was my first experience making hard decisions on understanding your business and your business model, and then making appropriate operating expense cuts. I'll never forget it. One of our board members—Mike Moritz, one of the most successful and famous venture capitalists in the world—sent out a sort of manual for surviving this period. It was a dense slide deck entitled "RIP Good Times." After a ton of stressful conversations with the CEO and the board, I recommended that I fire myself. There was no financial reason for me being on the payroll, and I also really didn't want to move to San Francisco, which was part of the original agreement when Shockwave bought us.

Just when I was feeling sorry for myself, I received a call from Rich Barton. At the time he was CEO of Expedia, which he had founded inside Microsoft and then spun out as a separate publicly traded company; he has gone on to found Zillow (where he is currently CEO), Glassdoor, and Avvo (which had a huge exit), and he is also a partner at blue-chip venture firm Benchmark Capital. He was calling me about a job reference, but in typical fashion, he pitched me on coming to Expedia.

It didn't take a lot of convincing. At Expedia I got to learn from wonderful leaders like Erik Blachford, Carrie Eiting, Lloyd Frink, Barney Harford, Bob Hohman, Spencer Rascoff, and so many others. It was like making the starting lineup of the Yankees in your second year as a pro. I took on the challenge of launching Expedia's corporate travel business, and I will pepper this book with examples from this experience. I learned how to grow a business from very small to very large—close to a billion dollars in sales. I didn't get everything right, but I learned a lot—not the least because the camaraderie and intellect around me created a very collegiate, meritocratic environment. The experience taught me how to focus on specific markets and customer targets, especially firmographic targeting—which is how B2B (business-to-business) companies segment their target market to discover their ideal customers. I also learned to really think big—Rich is the master of setting "Big Hairy Audacious Goals."

I have worked for some folks with very sharp elbows. Those sharp elbows definitely get your attention. Work with and for these people and you very quickly get an MBA on operating triage. But they also help you to see around every corner, so you learn to expect the next question before it's asked. When I was a young product manager, I had a very Pollyanna perspective on technology, because I never had to worry about making payroll or raising capital—I could just build awesome products for my customers. That perspective only lasted until I had to dig into the fundamentals of my business when it wasn't running well—and not just how the business worked, but also the market conditions and the overall marketplace we were in.

To make a long story short, I started to get a reputation for being an operator that took on turnarounds. A "man with a particular set of skills." From Expedia, I took on many turnarounds, from a failing startup called Mpire to a flailing public company (RealNetworks, for the second time) to a founder-owned, privately held marketplace business in Boise, Idaho. This work is not for the faint of heart. For instance, Mpire started out as an eBay reseller tool business—we turned it into an ad network called WidgetBucks, and then it became an ad tech company called AdXpose, which was sold to Comscore.

I wrote the first draft of this book during my tenure as president of the iconic language-learning company Rosetta Stone. Of all the turnarounds I talk about here, I like to think of Rosetta Stone as the most disciplined and satisfying, because we executed on a plan that created tremendous value for all constituents involved—from investors to employees to our customers—while helping learners around the world with their education goals. If you can have a role that does good by doing good, I can't think of a better personal mission for an aspiring business leader.

These experiences over multiple companies gave me a knack for pattern recognition that I will cover in this book. You'll also get a sense of my style. I don't take myself too seriously; I like to have fun. I'm very passionate about what I do. Most importantly, I realized early on that it's not the leader who makes a business successful; it's the team. All these stories and experiences were built on truly fantastic teams.

While there are many great business books on strategy, I wanted to write a different kind of strategy book—one that overlays a strategic framework with real-world lessons and stories from both my own experiences and those of other industry experts, to walk you through the five key questions to unlock value in your business. I will attempt to be very honest about areas in which I wasn't successful. As I've gotten older, I've learned what was important in my varied experiences. And I've gotten better at making decisions.

If you take away one thing from this book, let it be this: You need a plan. That is easy to say, but how do you create it? My hope is that with this book in hand, you can determine if your business has the potential to change its trajectory, whether you are at the helm of a cash cow or a startup.

Giddy-up!

WHAT IS THE
INSIGHT SCORE?

THIS BOOK WALKS you (the business leader) through five key questions that will help you determine whether you can unlock value for your company. Instead of wasting dollars and time on an entire strategic planning process, which typically takes months and/or large sums of money paid to a consulting group, this exercise can be condensed into five core questions that will help determine if a company's market position can be changed.

I'll take you through each question and inject my own insights with real-world examples. I will add perspectives from other thought leaders and CEOs too. What I hope you achieve is a view of your path ahead so that you can have a balanced win. This is so important to me because some of the most wonderful experiences of my career have been when we have seen a balanced expression of results—not just financial results but results where everyone wins: customers, investors, employees, and society.

This is a very simple calculation for a very complicated topic. I have used this format for every turnaround I have undertaken. Is it flawless? No. Is it a helpful guide? Well, you tell me. One thing is for sure, though—reading this book and thinking through the exercises and how they apply to your business will be a lot cheaper than paying for an expensive consulting firm. Once you see that black American Express card and the sleek designer business attire, you are screwed!

At the end of each of the five sections, you will be asked to score your response. Think of the Insight Score like your credit score, a weighted calculation that takes aspects of your past and present credit history to determine your creditworthiness. The Insight Score acts in the same way. The equation is simple. You add up the values from questions 1 to 4 and then multiply them by question 5.

Each question maps to one of the five sections in the book. You can use this book to supplant your strategic planning process. I remember the Insight Score simply as the acronym TTTPM (TAM, Timing, Track Record, Plan, and Momentum). Or if you want to be hip, it's T3PM.

Here is an overview of the questions:

Is the market big and growing? This helps you identify if the total addressable market (TAM) is large enough for your business to grow.

How to score this question:

- It's still emerging/undefined. (1 pt.)
- It's a <$1 billion market. (2 pts.)
- It's a large, $1-billion-plus market. (3 pts.)

Are the dynamics of the market favorable to you? This is about timing of market entry and whether the right conditions exist for you to win. Timing is the hardest question to answer, especially if you're an early-stage company. You are often too early or too late if you're a newer player.

How to score this question:

- It's unclear. (1 pt.)
- It's shifting in our favor. (2 pts.)
- Yup. It's good for us. (3 pts.)

Do you have a good track record in this space? You'll know if you have product/market fit. You'll have a good sense of your momentum getting customers, working with suppliers, beating the competition, etc.

How to score this question:

- It's slow going—too soon to tell. (1 pt.)
- We have a strong fit. (2 pts.)
- We have an advantage. (3 pts.)

Do you have an executable plan? In my experience, when I'm taking over a company, this is typically lacking. If you are in the right place at the right time and have an offering that is working in the marketplace, that's more than half the battle— but you need a strategic plan. I often find that in turnaround situations, there's a strategy issue—for example, a company is working on too many businesses or has too many priorities.

How to score this question:

- Not yet, still working on it. (1 pt.)
- Got a plan, no resources. (2 pts.)
- We are ready to *go*! (3 pts.)

How confident are you that you can attract the talent and resources needed to pull this off? Sometimes, you're in a business that may not be attractive for new capital. Typically, if you are getting higher numbers for the first three questions, you have a business that investors should be interested in, and it will be easier to attract and retain talent.

How to score this question:

- Not at all. (1 pt.)
- Pretty confident. (2 pts.)
- Very. No problem! (3 pts.)

Remember to multiply the total from questions 1 to 4 by the total from question 5. I've seen high degrees of success if the score is over 24. Anything over 30 is a no-brainer with a high likelihood of success. You typically want to be very confident that you are in a big market with great timing. It's OK if you don't have the right plan or the perfect product yet, assuming that you have the ability to attract the right team and capital. Not every business is a scaled market leader or has an edge that delivers high returns to investors. That's OK. A string of laundromats is very different from a software startup, but both can be viable businesses.

The final score is a guide for you. I would encourage you to really probe in areas that you feel are the "tweeners." What I mean by this is that you should question a score where your operator "Spidey sense" is tingling. You know what I mean; it's those decisions where you are not quite sure. There are some useful ways to get into the real truth behind each score throughout this book. Providing a score to a business is difficult to do, and business is a team sport. You will be better served by being more inclusive in your assessment, to remove any bias. If you think about it, this makes a ton of sense. It's like giving yourself a personal grade on a test—you cannot be as objective. But in general, you want to have the highest score possible. Here is a graphic guide for you:

What Is a Good Insight Score?

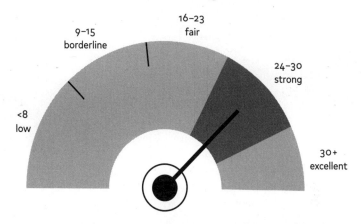

I hope you enjoy getting some color in each of the sections. You can skip the Insight Score if you'd like and just read through the different sections in order to pull out an insight or two as part of your strategic planning process.

Happy planning, and good luck with your growth strategy!

ONE

ALIGNMENT TO MARKET GROWTH TRENDS

INSIGHT QUESTION #1

Is your TAM
(total addressable market)
large enough?

1

MARKET DEFINITION

Is the Market Big and Growing?

There's a common adage that you need at least a billion-dollar market to make an exciting business. That is not necessarily true for all businesses—it's totally fine to own and run a small, cash flow–positive company. However, the sentiment is definitely true if you are looking to be a venture capital–based business or any business that has "scaled" long-term growth prospects. We are talking about a business that has the potential to be or is over $100 million. This is because you need to ensure that you have enough clearance in your market to grow market share and support your long-term growth. If you are looking for capital with investors, they are going to want to ensure the market is large enough to support your valuation so that they can get a reasonable return.

So, to reiterate, a $1-billion-plus addressable market is important because you need a high enough ceiling in a marketplace to operate. If your market is small and crowded, you're going to have compression. The market may be attractive, but that compression inevitably means that you will have new and existing entrants all competing for your customers, suppliers, leads, etc. For instance, if you are relying on paid installs or paid traffic for customer acquisition, the competition will continually drive up your costs as activity intensifies. I have seen this time and time again, from shopping marketplaces to travel. I once ran a gaming business, and there we saw that having size and scale ensured that our company had better margins and could outprice the competition.

In all these matters, the situation gets worse with a smaller market. Your upside is capped (because it's small), and the market becomes inefficient over time. It's a lot easier to operate in a larger market with several different types of serviceable, addressable markets—a subject we will get into in the next chapter.

Big TAM but Where Are You Servicing It?

First of all, you need a big total addressable market or TAM. But you also need a large and growing serviceable market. The SAM—serviceable addressable market—is where your company or products address a set of customers. It's rare to have a SAM that is as large as your TAM. Identifying an addressable market where you can have some competitive advantage is important, especially if you can find a SAM that is growing faster than the overall market. This is a great opportunity to get an edge in the marketplace. It's a good place to knock down your first proverbial bowling pin.

Understanding your SAM enables you to focus and get a wedge into the market. It's a great place to start. There are several ways to look at the market. You can look at how you're growing against the overall size of the market, which can be unit market share or as a revenue leader. Or you can compare your performance against the TAM and SAM to see how your relative performance is tracking.

I'm always surprised to see entrepreneurs talk about their total addressable market without understanding who they're targeting within that market. In the B2B space, you are typically targeting via firmographics to slice up your TAM and SAM. In the consumer space, it is typically both demographics and psychographics for determining your target.

In fact, when I worked at IAC (InterActiveCorp, a holding company that is the mastermind of media and e-commerce mogul Barry Diller), we literally just talked to a version of the following diagram. You have to look at the TAM, the SAM, and what percentage of each market you can obtain. Those three numbers mapped over time should give you a strong sense of whether you have found a compelling business proposition with a large enough operating pond.

Total Addressable Market

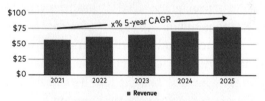

Service Addressable Market

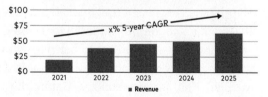

CAGR: compound annual growth rate

Your Forecasted Growth & Market Share

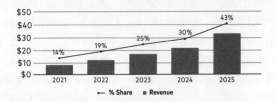

I really want to stress the importance of starting off your analysis by being very clear on your TAM and your SAM. Use these diagrams to help you. I have included several examples with some colorful stories to better illustrate the point from an operator's perspective.

Case Study: Mpire—The Empire Was Too Small

Identifying a compelling problem to solve is certainly important. But I can't stress enough the need to pick a compelling *addressable* market. A good example of picking the right market and the right problem to solve is a business called Mpire.

Mpire was founded by two friends of mine. I was initially asked to be a board member before I came in as CEO. The company built a very cool ERP (enterprise resource planning) system for eBay buyers. The thought behind the platform was to make it super easy for anyone to build a business. The focus was on eBay, but the idea was to eventually build APIs (application programming interfaces), which are like Lego blocks that allow applications to connect to each other and to other e-commerce platforms. Remember that this is pre-Shopify. Mpire raised money from a Seattle-based venture capital firm called Ignition Partners. Dave Cotter (the founding CEO) had built an awesome vision for the company—what he called the "American Dream 2.0." The idea was to enable anyone to build a business, using eBay as the first pre-existing marketplace to do this.

Besides the obvious threat of building a business on top of another business, Mpire had a great product, great investors, and a great team, but the TAM was just too small. To break this down, the eBay seller tools marketplace already had a lot of competition in it. eBay also had their own product. The players that were in it didn't really build large, successful businesses, which is an obvious red flag. In addition, the competitors selling tools in the space moved up-market, meaning they went after larger eBay buyers.

Think of these buyers as the eBay equivalent of the S&P 500. Mpire was focused on smaller buyers—or, to extend the analogy, the small-cap players in the eBay ecosystem. And overall, eBay didn't have a strong and thriving ecosystem. The golden rule for successful platform businesses is that the players who build products on top of the platform—not the platform itself—capture the lion's share of the value. eBay did not have a thriving marketplace strategy for developers—it was capturing the main sources of value in the ecosystem itself. When we analyzed the TAM (the eBay seller tool business) and the SAM (small business eBay), along with the percentage of that SAM that we could reach, we found we had what you could affectionately call market-sizing "mice nuts." There simply wasn't a lot of room to grow the business, let alone build a compelling venture-based business model.

I remember saying in my first board meeting for Mpire that we were selling productivity software to people who don't value their time. Yikes. Welcome to the board. What to do when you are in a crowded and small addressable market? Well, you pivot. Which is what we did—we pivoted the company to a bigger TAM. Here's how.

B2B Case Study: Mpire to WidgetBucks to AdXpose, Oh My! Pivoting to a Bigger TAM.

So, like I said, we pivoted. In fact, we pivoted twice—which I do not recommend because you waste investors' capital, but we were running out of money. Fast.

As background, Mpire's relationship with eBay was really strong. We had been one of their favorite third-party developers. We were using their eBay seller data API to pull out some interesting insights. The use case was originally using that data for sellers to automate the process of pricing their listings and knowing how to price them. This was hard because eBay's data was completely unstructured. We had access to the API and were able to make sense of this unstructured data, better than eBay in some cases. We actually figured out how to build a better eBay search engine than eBay could. We built custom algorithms specifically for eBay's customer data set. eBay has a leafless structure, meaning you can post any product, such as a shirt, and not necessarily have to map it to the sort of taxonomy you would normally see (like Shirts>Men> Size>Color>Brand). It's not like Amazon. An eBay seller enters their own listing and can put it in any category. So the ability for a consumer to navigate a crisp taxonomy is difficult, and some consumers couldn't find certain products because they were misclassified. Mpire figured out a way to make sense of all this noise in the data.

eBay was interested in working with us. We didn't like the idea of custom projects, but we needed cash to keep the company going. Our first project was to build a custom merchandising module on eBay.com, which we called eBay Pop. It was a dynamic search application that was hosted by us, but it looked to consumers like it was hosted by eBay. These types of multi-application integrations using APIs were later popularized in the Web 2.0 vernacular as "widgets."

We created a very cool search engine inside of eBay that culled through all their data to find trending products and highly relevant trending items on eBay. We could horizontally look across eBay and dissect trends across their entire data set. eBay was blown away by this. The head of eBay collectibles at the time, Lo Toney, who is now a very successful venture capitalist, literally kept our business alive with this project.

We hosted the app ourselves and were able to keep all the IP around our work—the concept and code behind eBay Pop was ours. We were hoping that we could end up selling the technology (and the company) to eBay. But that didn't happen. There was a CEO change (Meg Whitman to John Donahoe), and other priorities moved into the foreground.

The feature we had built for eBay worked really well. They wanted us to do more and asked us to create an ad network for them. eBay already had a very successful affiliate business, but they were interested in expanding their platform outside of eBay. They saw that Mpire could build very contextual, highly engaging ads. So we created "shopping ads" as a way for eBay to better merchandise their listings—in essence, merchandising "widgets." These were designed to scour a page and extract keywords using our custom algorithm. I called this Product Sense, a name that was a lame rip-off of Google's AdSense business. It was a play on Google's contextualization ad capability.

With our work for eBay completed and no prospects to sell the company, we started to think about what we should be doing next. We had some assets, a good team, and access to all of eBay's seller data. We could present the data in unique and creative ways that customers loved and that increased conversion—and we could do this better than anyone else in the market. We even started to build a consumer shopping site, but creating a product search engine from scratch with a team that had no direct-to-consumer experience *and* little venture capital didn't seem like a great idea.

Our pivot really exemplified the thinking in this book. We didn't have the luxury of time, since we were running out of capital and options, so we decided to do a sort of agile sprint version of our strategic plan. The team and I went back to the drawing board and thought carefully about the eBay Pop concept and the ad network idea. We had no idea how to run an ad network. But at that time there were a couple of things happening in the marketplace. It was the dawn of Web 2.0, and the concept of bite-sized components powering other applications across the Internet was just starting to take off. These applications powered by APIs or widgets were just starting to get excitement and, most importantly to us at the time, investor interest.

Widgets were hot. When we evaluated the market, we realized that with the proliferation of user-generated content, blogs, etc., there was a need for unique ad inventory. Ad networks sold crappy ads that no one looked at, and there were a lot of them entering the market. In addition to the eight-hundred-pound gorilla Google, everyone wanted to build new monetization for these smaller types of publishers. There was a desire for publishers to provide more experiences that were more customized and personalized to their audiences. We had already built most of the core tech to provide some awesome experiences.

When we looked at the market, I thought we would be able to build a superior experience for the publisher that would also delight the consumer. We thought that by using the same tech that eBay had literally paid us to build for them, we would be able to go to market very quickly. Going back to the lesson in this chapter, we looked at the advertising TAM, and it was huge. The SAM was also huge (ad display networks versus the entire industry), and our ability to penetrate the market had promise. So we built an ad network.

We called that company WidgetBucks. Yes, it was the most blatantly obvious name to muster any future potential M&A (mergers and acquisitions) interest. But heck, we had an existing investor that wanted to see something happen with their investment, along with a smart and pliable team of ten employees.

I found (because I was the CEO, head of sales, and chief bottle washer) that smaller publishers didn't get the attention of larger advertisers. Smaller publishers relied on ad networks that aggregated inventory on behalf of their ad suppliers. The ad network splits the monetization with the publishers and themselves. I talked to larger publishers, but I was consistently measured against premium ad placements, and they wanted guarantees. In the long-tail publisher space (aka super-low-trafficked websites) at the time, there was a small number of affiliate market gurus who everyone listened to and who, most importantly, drove action in trialing new ad products. They moved a ton of impressions across a large set of publishers. I decided to target these individuals, who were a cross between the personalities you would see selling direct-to-consumer products via TV ads late at night (when inventory is cheap) and technical hackers.

We launched an MVP (minimum viable product), an admin tool, and a publishing interface. We built out the infrastructure and scale. And our ad units—oh my. Our ad units were beautiful. They were Flash based, which made them interactive (you could literally shop inside the ad unit); they were small (they didn't slow down websites); and publishers loved them.

The reason publishers loved our product was because if, for example, you were a passionate do-it-yourself PC gamer blogger, our ads would just look at your page and magically identify and contextualize the content and then show relevant products that consumers could buy. The ads looked like content, *and* the publishers could get a cut of the sales. We also started to think through how we could attach supply that we didn't source to shopping without doing that work ourselves. We would be the middleman that drove demand throughout the publisher network. We started with eBay content and then Amazon. We then targeted popular e-commerce shopping networks like Shopping.com, PriceGrabber.com, Shopzilla, and others. They supplied cost-per-click-based advertising, which provided more immediate monetization than advertising that relied on a cost-per-action (an actual sale). The CPC model is great, as long as you provide quality traffic, which is what ended up hurting us.

We wanted to launch big, so we targeted the popular affiliate marketing show Affiliate Summit. Since we were going after several of the largest influencers, I thought that we should appeal to their hubris and their desire to make money without doing much work. We created custom baseball cards for each of the affiliate marketers, with the affiliate mogul's face on the front over their earnings statistics, like their average Google AdWords' monthly commission. I then created an incentive for them to promote us, a super affiliate model where each new publisher would get a small revenue share whenever they generated revenue. This worked. Perhaps too well. Literally overnight, we became a top-twenty advertising network as reported by Comscore, and we were soon serving billions of impressions. Everyone from the industry to investors was asking themselves, "Who the hell are these guys?"

With this newfound growth, we looked for new capital and eventually raised $10 million from Draper Fisher Jurvetson. We literally had investors waiting in our lobby, and I made sure to display our growth charts there on live wall monitors so they could stare at the real-time exponential growth while they were waiting. We also started to think about new verticals to go after with our innovative ad idea. Travel was next up. We closed the round, and growth was insane.

But we didn't realize what we had unleashed. We launched another MVP as a large release, but by then our network was being infiltrated by nefarious ad players, individuals, and organizations. The quality of the traffic was very low, and I had to play a game of whack-a-mole as advertiser after advertiser turned us off because of the horrible traffic. I remember a conversation with an advertiser, which took place right as I was about to enjoy a nice vacation in Napa Valley, that went something like this: "Matt, I like you. I like your product. This is the last check that I am going to write to you. This check is for $300,000. For all the traffic that you have sent us, our advertisers have made no money."

I went through a series of deals with new partners and even decided to show a banner ad (powered by new display ad networks), but the quality was eventually so bad that we knew we had a problem. Our thoughts on market sizing were right, and I could argue that if we had approached the business with less capital, we would have launched differently, but we were now in a very bad position of needing to pay publishers while advertisers were turning us off.

So we had to pivot... again. I won't go into that story too much. But we had built an awesome product, in a big market, with the right product fit, and we were despondent. The original CTO and co-founder of Mpire, Greg Harrison, was so upset that he started to think through how we could stop the bad guys in the advertising space. The ad networks and exchanges were not doing anything to stop fraud. There was a tremendous amount of wasted spend (paying for ads that were never seen), as well as advertising that was not brand aligned showing up on publishers' sites (like top-tier brand advertisers popping up on porn sites). Greg turned his rage into action. He instilled this crazy passion for providing truth and justice in advertising. It turns out that we had inherently built the capability for a new product and our next pivot.

I don't recommend pivoting so quickly back-to-back. But, again, we didn't have a lot of options, and once you take venture capital, you are on a road to growth (or ruin). After sitting around the kitchen table and deciding on a new name for the business that was basically a play on "exposing" the fact that there was a tremendous amount of fraud and waste in the online advertising space, we launched AdXpose as a software-as-a-service product for agencies, brands, networks, and exchanges. I wish I could say it was one of those incredible home runs. But it wasn't, from an IRR (internal rate of return) perspective. The fact that we had any IRR for investors was amazing, but the early investors didn't get any upside. I had hired some fantastic business leaders in CEO Kirby Winfield and CFO Jeff Bergstrom, who both know startups. These folks took AdXpose to another level.

We also assembled a fantastic board for this type of advertising business, and that includes investors, notably Bill Bryant from DFJ; Mike Vernon of Zulily and aQuantive; and Jeff Lanctot, former chief strategy officer of Razorfish. We also had some notable board members, like Rob Solomon (who had just recently left Groupon) and Michelle Goldberg and Rich Tong of Ignition Partners.

We went after a sub-billion-dollar eBay seller tool business, and we stepped back and took the same team and expertise but looked at a larger multibillion-dollar ad business. The path to building AdXpose—which eventually sold to Comscore for $22 million—was definitely not a straight one.

Looking back, I can see that this was a successful turnaround. However, our early investors didn't get a great return, and our later-stage investor certainly didn't make venture-style returns. We inevitably built a business that generated a ton of value at Comscore—and to be clear, I was not operating the business at the time of the acquisition (but I remained on the board). Credit goes to the operating team, many of whom stayed on through the acquisitions.

The business generated $100 million in annual recurring revenue (ARR), but we wasted a ton of money with these pivots. I was recently asked how many pivots are too many. Honestly, I don't have any hard data on this. But as a rule of thumb, I would say you should only be doing one pivot from your original business idea.

B2B Case Study: Building a Big Business at Expedia

Another example of looking at the TAM and SAM is my experience at Expedia. Today, Expedia is a $22-billion-plus publicly traded online travel e-commerce juggernaut. I joined the company right after September 11, 2001. I was just coming off a difficult startup experience and was looking to do something from the ground floor but at a bigger company. As you may recall from the introduction, I had to cut a lot of costs and people at the startup for it to survive.

Travel is one of those monster categories that never ceases to innovate. The global category is over $9 trillion, and online travel alone is over $300 billion. Just when you think there isn't any more innovation, another new startup brings a new twist to this mongo market. It reminds me of the patent office quote that "everything that can be invented has been invented."

I started at Expedia as the lone employee tasked with building a B2B business. Expedia was and still is primarily a consumer business. They'd had a couple of unsuccessful attempts at the corporate travel space prior to my arrival. One of these had been a partnership with American Express, which is not only one of the largest credit card companies but at the time was also the largest seller of travel (especially corporate travel) in the world. That partnership went horribly wrong, in a way that reminded me of when Microsoft tried working with IBM. IBM wanted Microsoft to build a graphics-based operating system called OS/2. Microsoft built its own system called Windows as an upgrade to DOS. Windows became the focus, and OS/2 became a dud because of Microsoft's focus on their own OS. That is sort of how it went down at Expedia. American Express wanted to white label Expedia for their corporate needs, but Expedia really wanted to focus its energy on a direct-to-consumer play versus a white label (where the customer doesn't realize that Expedia is powering the experience) or OEM play (an "original equipment manufacturer," where a company produces a product to be marketed by another company).

Travel is a size and scale game. There are lots of intermediaries and lots of services: hotels, cars, air, destination services, etc. Expedia had only focused on consumers, which is about half the market. The other half is corporate travel. I helped launch the online corporate travel business, Expedia Corporate Travel, now known as Egencia.

Given that it's half the travel business, one would expect to see more innovation in this space. The larger travel management companies control most business travel spend; when we were launching Expedia Corporate Travel twenty years ago, the top six agencies (American Express, Carlson Wagonlit Travel, etc.) controlled three-quarters of the gross bookings market. This is what the market looked like. At the time, it was around $260 billion in the US, and much larger worldwide.

The main features then were:

• Fortune 2000 (employee size over twenty thousand) made up approximately 35 percent of the travel spend.

• Large enterprises (employee size between fourteen thousand and twenty thousand) made up approximately 30 percent of the travel spend; this is over ten thousand companies.

• Medium-sized businesses (employee size between one hundred and two thousand) made up approximately 25 percent of the travel spend; this is about 100,000 companies.

• Small-sized businesses (employee size between one and ninety-nine) made up approximately 10 percent of the travel spend; this is about seven million companies.

It's simple, right? Go after the top enterprises and close them just like a consumer business. Going back to our previous work on the TAM and SAM, we can break down an approach that gives us initial "successful" product/market fit. It's too easy for a budding entrepreneur to look at a big market and say, "Why don't we just target everyone in the market-place?" When you look at TAM and SAM, it's also important to look at your entry points. For consumer businesses, it could be demographic and psychographic information. Say you want to target female health and wellness aficionados that are between twenty-five and forty-five and have college degrees and care about social issues. You would go to market with different propositions and positioning than if you were targeting stay-at-home moms. Every market has an entry point, and every persona and firm have different wants and needs.

For this case study, we are talking about B2B. For B2B you have to think about the size of the firm (which drives the type of buyer and budget) as well as the firmographic. Firmographics are specific attributes that enable you to target companies. It can be the size of the firm (by revenue and employees), the vertical (defined by what is called a SIC (Standard Industrial Classification) code), and even geography.

Bringing it back to this example, we realized that we had a couple of hurdles. One, Expedia was known as a consumer brand, not an enterprise brand. We knew that we would not be taken too seriously by larger companies. We also knew that the larger enterprises wanted a lot of customization to their product. Later, I will walk through in more detail how we looked at the supply side of our business. Online booking was also very new at the time, and most corporations were still using off-line travel agents.

Our plan was to build a product that had company-specific content (their own negotiated rates) as well as Expedia's significant arsenal of its own content. We wanted to be the market maker with suppliers by pooling our scale to negotiate better rates on behalf of thousands of smaller businesses. We looked at all the conditions in the market and realized that the largest corporate clients would kill us with custom requirements and their low-margin-minded current customers, the traditional corporate travel companies. "Low-margin-minded" means fee-based, usage compensation—and lower profit margins.

After much analysis and testing with customers, we found that our proposition really worked for companies that were technology-centric (like technical and software companies) *and* not large enough to have a lot of negotiated rates. They needed Expedia's content to supplant their own size. This enabled us to focus on several verticals in the mid-market, and we were able to get feedback on our business without having to become defocused on the wants and needs of every customer. It also enabled us to focus our efforts on having a clear value proposition while avoiding an expensive battle competing against large players that had been in the market for thirty-plus years.

So let's break this down. Our analysis went from a larger total TAM in the corporate travel space to a SAM in the mid-market, and then to a more focused strategy of zooming in on a couple of verticals. Getting this clear in your market entry enables you to define a clear product and proposition on which to focus and become successful. You can then expand into other verticals and firmographics over time. This strategy is clearly defined in one of my favorite business books, *Crossing the Chasm*. The author, Geoffrey A. Moore, discusses the importance of a bowling pin strategy: focusing on your initial customer and then expanding from there in order to knock down the rest of the bowling pins. That is the only way to get a strike in a marketplace. You can knock all the bowling pins down in a market by focusing only on the front row.

As a side note, we also decided to buy a small corporate travel agency. It was based in Seattle and had a good swath of small and world-class clients like Amazon, Starbucks, and Nordstrom. The business, Metropolitan Travel, enabled us to learn how we could service larger customers and build technology to run a traditional business more efficiently. For example, features that were traditionally done by agents manually (for a fee), like upgrading a customer to first class, were eventually integrated into our software. For free. This gave our solution a substantial competitive advantage, since we owned the software, and other corporate travel agencies had to license their software from other vendors (e.g., Sabre's GetThere).

Case Study: Romancing the Stone

Here's another example. You might have heard of Rosetta Stone—pioneers who created the world's first digital language-learning software. I joined the business in 2017 when the company was struggling to keep up with the times. Heck, it was basically still a perpetual software business.

What does this have to do with the total addressable market? Well, most of the investment in the language business was focused on the enterprise language-learning space. This market is much smaller than the consumer, K to 12, and kids' markets. The company had focused on this segment because they believed that they weren't going to be successful in the direct-to-consumer space. There was concern about Duolingo's free product, which they feared was going to eat up all the market share. So the strategy was largely defensive. To set the context, the addressable market for language learning is around $50 billion a year. The penetration of this market by digital products is still single digit. There are a lot of geographical differences as well as customer segments in the space, and you have to be very judicious to find your edge and market entry point.

It was clear that we were not very good at B2B and it was a smaller addressable market. We did a top-to-bottom review of the business in about ninety days and determined that the consumer market, especially in the US, was a better place to start. We also had ignored one of our biggest advantages: the brand. Rosetta Stone has 90-plus-percent brand awareness in the US. Despite this, we were not focused on the consumer at all. The team also did a ton of great customer research to ensure that we were validating our intuition concerning where to focus the business.

The way we approached it was to not *just* look at the TAM and SAM. We also wanted to identify any competitive advantage—and the main one was our brand. Once we locked in on the US language-learning market (which is about 20 percent of the overall market, with single-digits digital penetration), we then started to look at our market entry point. Our brand really stands for the gold standard in the space (or is it cooler to say the "Bitcoin standard"?). We wanted to identify a consumer segment that resonated with our brand attributes of being a premium and effective product.

Here is how we sliced up the market by psychographics. We looked at the North America language SAM and then did some deep customer research that showed there was a subset of this market that was perfect for our offering. Within this segment (which we nicknamed the Expressives), we identified three subsegments. Each had a different gender and personal bias, but all those segments were keen on our premium offering (I won't go into much detail on these segments—it's pretty proprietary).

Let's take a detour for a second and do a little Strategy 101 overview from the guru of strategy, Michael Porter. In his book *Competitive Advantage: Creating and Sustaining Superior Performance*, Porter says that for a horizontal (mass market) product, you have two possible strategies: a low-cost horizontal strategy or a premium differentiated strategy. We chose the latter. The chart showing these strategies is deceptively simple because it makes sure that you build out competitive advantages that will allow you to create defensible long-term value. Those consumers we call Expressives are willing to pay for a premium branded experience. We found that in the US, there were 65 million Expressives out of 165 million people who were the right opportunity for us.

Porter's Generic Strategies

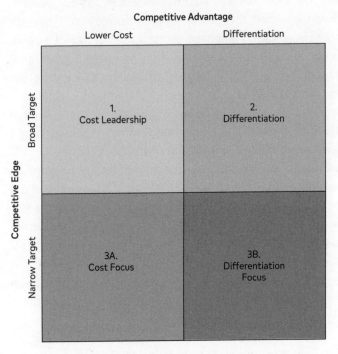

MICHAEL PORTER, *COMPETITIVE ADVANTAGE*, 1985

Because we focused the strategy on creating a premium experience for our customers, our benchmark was never the number of subscribers or units; it was the highest lifetime value (LTV) growing at or above the revenue share growth rate. I ceded the unit share leadership to the low-cost differentiated competitor. There are free products like Duolingo that will naturally pursue that strategy. We can debate whether Amazon's adage that "your margin is my opportunity" is correct, but I personally believe that a clear differentiated strategy with a brand that is aligned (with the right position and pricing) can be and has been a winning strategy. The point is to identify how you're targeting the market—not just the whole addressable market but the part of the market that is serviceable. That enables you to delineate between features pricing and packaging and identify the right customer wants and needs for the particular market you're going after.

KEY TAKEAWAYS FROM THIS CHAPTER

To assess whether your addressable market is attractive to start and grow a business, consider the following key high-lights from this chapter:

- Ideally, you need a $1-billion-plus TAM. To have larger returns, you will need to take an honest look at the market you are playing in. You have a better chance of succeeding with an addressable market that is over a billion dollars. Taking an honest look at your market is the initial step to determine if you have an opportunity to unlock value in your business.

- What is the customer pain? You need to frame the market pain that you are going to address and what market is being addressed. Investors are looking for a TAM that is large enough that the small percentage of the market share that your company addresses could make an interesting business. If you are presenting an opportunity where in five years your $20 million in revenue equates to 50 percent of the TAM, then this is just too small. Investors will typically want you to have a healthy revenue line in five years, equating to single-digit market share.

- You can always make refinements to your go-to-market plan, but you can't fake the size of the market. If the market is undefined or emerging, then you may be able to get away with not having a billion-dollar market. However, a large market that is growing or a pre-existing market that is ripe for disintermediation are the situations that are primed for unlocking large value opportunities.

- Do your homework. In your business plan, show the overall market opportunity by building out the market segmentation (by demographic, psychographic, SIC code, etc.). Get as granular as possible. Layer in specific detail on segmentation growth rates, if possible.

HOW WOULD YOU SCORE THIS SECTION?

It's time to score your first piece to the Insight Score on TAM. This question is identifying if the TAM is large enough for your business to grow. This should be the easiest question for you to answer because in many cases the data is public, clear, and less likely to be fungible.

INSIGHT QUESTION #1
Is your TAM (total addressable market) large enough?

How to score this question:

- It's still emerging/undefined. (1 pt.)
- It's a <$1 billion market. (2 pts.)
- It's a large, $1-billion-plus market. (3 pts.)

On to the next question!

TWO

TIMING

INSIGHT QUESTION #2

Timing. Are the dynamics
of the market
favorable to you?

2

TIMING IS
EVERYTHING

NOW THAT WE'VE discussed the total addressable market, let's talk about its cousin—timing. Of the five variables in the Insight Score, "timing" and TAM are the most important because they are out of your control. They are conditions that happen to you whether you like them or not.

We have all heard the salacious comment, "Size doesn't matter." Well, we just got done talking about TAM. While size does matter for the reasons we described in that section, I would argue that timing matters more. Timing is the single most difficult attribute to score and to gauge, the most elusive. When I put together my thoughts for the Insight Score and this book, I left this section for last, because it's so difficult. I also struggled with whether I was giving timing the adequate multiplier value because of its importance. However, if you don't have capital, a large enough market, etc., then the timing is generally moot, so I decided to give timing the same multiplier as the other variables.

I have been on both the wrong side and the right side of timing many times in my career. I have already referenced an entertainment company, AtomFilms, that I helped to found. The founder, Mika Salmi, had a great idea—short-form entertainment over the burgeoning new Internet. We dreamed of the Internet as a mass medium for a new form of entertainment experience for millions of consumers. We were right with this idea, clearly—but we were a bit early. Most consumers were still accessing the Internet over dial-up connections. Just a short time later a company called YouTube started out with user-generated content and a frictionless way for consumers (using Flash) to create and upload their content. It's interesting to note that both AtomFilms and YouTube shared the same iconic investor, Mike Moritz of famed venture capital institution Sequoia Capital. AtomFilms was founded in 1998, and YouTube launched in 2005. AtomFilms did have a liquidity event many years later at an OK but not great return for investors, while YouTube had a $1.65 billion exit and subsequently generated billions in enterprise value for Google. Timing is a bitch.

In the technology space, there are so many examples. The biggest winners made an early bet, either through luck or a key insight, around either a behavioral change, a technology change, or both. Here are some of those examples:

Dial-up to broadband. This gave rise to massive Web 1.0 businesses that took advantage of the higher bandwidth. No more AOL (which was a popular dial-up Internet service, in case you are too young to remember).

PC to mobile computing. Think of any mobile company that you use today. I remember 1999, the year my youngest daughter was born—and the year I started using a service called Kozmo. I could buy a can of Coke at one in the morning, and it would be delivered to my door for a miniscule service fee. The unit economics didn't make sense at the time. Fast-forward to today with Uber Eats or Postmates. Same idea. Different form factor and different economics.

Mobile feature phone to smartphone. A new form factor gave rise to mobile-specific experiences that changed the world forever. Think transportation (Uber) to gaming (Rovio).

On-premise to cloud storage. Think of the rise of Amazon cloud services, open-source databases, etc. No more expensive hardware to purchase. All that infrastructure is now rented versus owned.

You don't want to be too early, which is a common issue with companies of any size trying to enter a new market. It's actually easier to determine if you are too late than too early. There are several pieces of timing, and I'd like to differentiate between two key components: either focus on a small but growing market or identify a technology or behavior change.

Pick a Small but Growing Market

There are lots of ways to enter one of these new markets. But there's typically one commonality. To have the best chance at success and timing, you need to be pursuing a small market that's growing very quickly. If you think about it, it makes sense: if you're focusing on a small market that's not growing fast or it's too early, you won't have a sense of whether you should be entering the market. On the flip side, if it's too big and there's already a lot of market entrants, then you have to assume that the world's best minds have optimized the heck out of it already. It will be expensive to acquire new customers, and entering this market will be very difficult. Of course, you can always have a new take on an existing market, which I think of as redefining an existing market as a small but growing market.

So, after you've done your work on the addressable market, look at opportunities based on your ability to get alpha or your ability to effect change using your existing resources, team, and momentum. You can actually enter a market that has existing competitors. There are many examples of companies that have redefined an existing market with a similar but different approach. Some examples:

Stripe. If you were honest with your past self, traveling back in time and looking at the fintech space, I seriously doubt that you would have predicted that Stripe would be such a dominant force in the payments industry. Stripe made payments super simple to implement and also targeted small but fast-growing companies, which gave it additional second-order effects in its growth. The company bet on the Internet economy.

Social networks. If you look at all the social networks around today, you'd be like that "everything that can be invented has been invented" comment that has been credited to the US patent office commissioner from 1899. Facebook started in 2004. What else could anyone do? Well, Instagram and Snapchat came about in 2010 and 2011. They had a new take on the market—a network based on images and another one focused on ephemeral filtered photos.

Here is a personal example from the days when I was involved with gaming. Many years ago, the CEO of the game company King (makers of the game *Candy Crush*) made a huge bet. I got acquainted with Riccardo Zacconi when I was running an online games business at RealNetworks. We were both in a similar spot. We had missed much of the big shift from downloadable PC games to social and mobile games. Riccardo had a successful cash-cow business that wasn't growing, and he was able to pivot the same team and resources into the company that we know and love today.

When I spoke with Riccardo on his decision to shift from PC games to social/mobile, he was clear to reiterate that King was not the first to market: "We [King] were not early to social. We experimented early on but only when we got disrupted by social; we had to focus all our resources on cracking how to bring our games to social as a matter of survival. It took two and a half years to crack Facebook and more than two hundred games and nine years before we launched *Candy Crush*, so more than luck, it took a lot of perseverance, passion, and hard work."

Riccardo's story is reminiscent of many conversations I have had with other founders and CEOs. Later in this chapter, you will hear eerily similar stories, like the one from Niklas Hed, co-founder of Rovio.

Another example of timing is Rosetta Stone, which I referenced in the first section. Making a model shift decision to both consumer and mobile applications meant not allocating capital to the other segments (corporate and K to 12) we were focused on. Earlier, we discussed why that was a good decision (e.g., larger TAM, good brand, etc.).

Again, it goes back to market definition. If you do find that your niche is very small and growing, you have a huge opportunity to exploit things that incumbents do not see.

Nearly every successful operator and founder will claim that their continued success is due to luck. But it's clear that they all have a strong sense of timing, a perspective based on macro market trends, and their own personal point of view that there's an opportunity that might be small but will grow very fast.

As another example of this, I spoke with Rob Solomon. Rob is the chairman of GoFundMe, the world's largest social fundraising platform. He has a long track record of successful market timing, having been at Yahoo! when the company was in its infancy (and joining it was not an obvious move), and having taken Groupon (at the time the most successful IPO in history) public as its president, as well as many other successful outcomes. In this interview, Rob initially talks about timing as luck. But very quickly, you will get a sense that Rob has a perspective on timing that has enabled him to select markets that will grow very, very fast.

What do you look at in terms of quantitative data to determine whether you are too late or too early in entering a new market?

I tend to look more at either qualitative or gut to really determine timing. I'll give you a couple of examples. My best timing ever was to join a company called Yahoo! My second-best timing ever was to join a company called Groupon. And the third-best timing ever was to join a company called GoFundMe. I think in all those examples, nobody [in my network] knew the rationale to what I was doing.

So back to the Yahoo! example. Yahoo! was this first Internet darling. A few "weird" people in Silicon Valley had joined the company—it was already a public company by the time I joined. Everyone in the world who I told I was going to work at Yahoo! was a little bit perplexed. This was way back in 1999 or so. And sure, the Internet was happening, but it really wasn't happening for most people, or they didn't really understand it. They'd check some new sport scores, or they'd screw around with email a little bit. But it wasn't a ubiquitous thing that had penetrated the world like we know today.

People weren't buying too many things; people were still very worried about entering their credit cards online.

So, when I joined Yahoo!, I just had this sense of, "This is a company that is really going to change the world." And when you look back, it really did; it was the company that created the blueprint that made it possible for the Facebooks and the Ubers and the Airbnbs and everyone else. It was this amazing brand that started taking over the world in that period. I was there from 1999 to 2005. I just had this sense that it was a special company. The founders were amazing; the group of people who were working there were making it up as we went. We were the sort of managers who didn't know how to manage a big, global-scaled Internet company. They would throw challenges at people, and we'd all figure it out.

Timing-wise, that was the best thing that got me into the Internet. It helped me to understand what it would take to build special companies. And the people who were at Yahoo! from the beginning, if you look around now—they're everywhere. They're running venture capital firms; they're the most important people at companies like Airbnb and Uber— you name it. It was the place; we all grew up as managers on the Internet. So that was one example of timing, just getting it so right, but not knowing why—I didn't have any data, really; I just had this feeling that the Internet was going to be important. And Yahoo! was going to be an important company.

So then on to Groupon. Groupon was a very interesting company; it was formed in Chicago, and back then, in 2008 to 2010, there weren't a lot of great companies being formed outside of Silicon Valley. There was Amazon [Seattle] and a handful of others. And out of Chicago, there's this company that is doing something pretty unique. It came up with a concept to get people from the Internet into physical retail locations, which was kind of blending and marrying online and off-line. And I interviewed Andrew Mason, the founder, and we hit it off. The company had about eighty people when I went there. And what was amazing was I told a lot of people, "I'm moving from Silicon Valley to Chicago to work at this company called Groupon." And they all looked at me like I was crazy, you know? "What is Groupon? Why would you do that?"

And what I realized was that off-line merchants were hurting pretty bad, small local merchants. They didn't have access to capital; the economy wasn't great, and they just needed customers. And what was magical about Groupon was that you can use the scale of the Internet to acquire tens of millions of customers. You could also be on the other side of the marketplace, bring on tens of thousands of merchants, and make them happy by giving them a cash infusion. So if you ran a Groupon, you raised a bunch of money right away, and that cash came in to you. And then you got a bunch of customers. And that was pretty profound. At the time, these off-line merchants needed customers, and they didn't know how to use the Internet to get them. We created a platform that could help them get customers.

And the timing on that was, again, not necessarily quantitative. What I realized was, here's a platform that can be the operating system for small businesses; it really had the opportunity to become that. So that was another example of timing, where a lot of solutions existed that were called local solutions. And what they really did was they gave people information about local businesses, but the local businesses who needed the customers weren't getting customers from the Internet at the time. And that's changed dramatically over the last decade. It was really lucky and fortuitous for me to be there at the beginning. And what happened at Groupon was that this idea was so powerful, it became the fastest-growing company in history. We may have made a few mistakes along the way. But it really was this amazing experience where I was one of the first one hundred employees; within twenty-four months, we were up to almost ten thousand people. And that had never happened up until that time. Now we see that with some other fast-growing companies, but it was pretty spectacular to be part of that.

Here's another example, where I joined the company back in 2015: GoFundMe. Not too many people had heard of the brand or the company. But what I realized was that the concept was incredibly powerful. We had millions of people who were being left behind, falling through the cracks of the existing social safety nets. The government wasn't there for them; NGOs weren't there for them. And then this weird platform where people could ask for help was starting to flourish. And if you fast-forward from 2015 to now, we're one of the largest giving organizations in the world. And it's a ubiquitous brand. Anytime something happens, whether it's an earthquake in Mexico or wildfires in California or a hurricane in the Southeast, people flock to GoFundMe when they need help. And what I realized from a timing perspective—then again, people scratched their heads and said, "What are you thinking, GoFundMe?"—I used to have to describe it as, "It's kind of like Kickstarter, but for causes." And today we're probably ten to twenty times larger than Kickstarter. So for me, timing is more about reading the tea leaves of what's possible and jumping into things.

So I am a little bit different than a lot of the quantitative wonks, who will use data and numbers to figure it out. I use more, you know, some market trends and consumer trends and my gut feeling about what technology can be doing for consumers.

Do you have an example of an experience where you entered a market correctly and where luck wasn't involved? Break down for us what, specifically, you did that made this experience successful.

Groupon. Groupon was a pretty good idea. It was this marketplace where you had consumers on one side who wanted access to great local businesses and great deals, and you had merchants on the other side who wanted customers. And if you think about every e-commerce business that has been created before 2010-ish, every single one of them grew up on the Google ecosystem. So if you weren't great at search engine optimization, search engine marketing, and a little bit of graphical ad buying on Google, you couldn't really thrive as an e-commerce business. And what was magical about the Groupon timing was Facebook was just starting to take off in a big way. And rather than grow up on the Google ecosystem, we used the Facebook ecosystem. We were probably the first global-scale player to do that, and what we realized was that Facebook had this ability for us to acquire customers by geography, by age group. And we could also acquire them much more cheaply than any other ecosystem out there. So we were at one point acquiring good customers on Facebook, in 2010 to 2011, for about $1 to $1.50 per customer. And these were customers who turned into buyers of Groupons.

If not for social media, specifically Facebook and their advertising capabilities, Groupon could not have thrived and flourished the way it did. So we could launch an offer in Chicago, targeted at twenty-five- to thirty-five-year-old women, find those customers really cheaply, and turn them into active buyers of Groupons, which made us happy and made our merchants incredibly happy. The timing here is that before the social ecosystems were created, I'm not sure Groupon could have happened if we were building it within the existing paradigms, but not for Facebook. Groupon may not have been able to scale the way it did—everywhere in thirty-plus countries. So the timing of this new business model, and this new social paradigm that was sweeping the world, allowed Groupon to become the fastest-growing company in history.

What are some hacks that you have learned over the years that have helped you determine whether you are entering a market at the right time?

Here's a great one. I thought GoFundMe was going to be a very typical e-commerce-like business or marketplace business where you could apply the traditional mechanics of how you build a marketplace, how you grow the marketplace, how you acquire customers. And we tried everything with the Google Ads we did—off-line television, radio, print ads. We did everything you could do to try and grow a marketplace. And if you look at every other marketplace that came before us, whether it be eBay or Uber or Airbnb, there was just a set of mechanics that everyone used that you could throw out with GoFundMe. We started trying everything, and we experimented, and things just didn't work the way they did in other marketplaces.

What we learned very quickly is that when people need access to capital and urgent need strikes, the traditional marketing methods don't work. And what we've learned over time with our GoFundMe campaigns is that the campaigns in and of themselves were very interesting. They were human-interest gold mines; we'd get a hundred thousand to two hundred thousand campaign starts every month, and probably 10 or 20 percent of them were super interesting to some audience. And what we started doing was taking those campaigns and amplifying them across any channel that wanted to see that content. So we built relationships with local news organizations, national news organizations, social media, email lists, you name it.

And what we built, instead of a traditional ad-buying machine or a search advertising machine to acquire customers, was what we call an "amplification machine" to acquire customers. So we would take our GoFundMe campaigns and scour them. We came up with some machine learning and artificial intelligence to figure out what might make for an interesting campaign. And then you really must have a human review component. We would find these interesting campaigns, and then we built probably the most effective and efficient PR machine in the history of technology. I'm almost certain that no company gets more coverage than GoFundMe. But it's not GoFundMe, the company. It's the *stories* that make up the GoFundMe fundraising campaigns.

So we spread them far and wide. And we've been in *People* magazine and on every morning show and every national news program. And we then expanded that on a global basis to do the same thing. So the hack here was that we couldn't find a way to get people to start campaigns and to help these campaigns grow, unless we invented a new way to do it. This "amplification machine" found interesting campaigns and spread them far and wide across the Internet.

And what's magical about that hack is it builds awareness for the GoFundMe brand, and it builds awareness for the campaign. And in building awareness for the campaign, more funds are raised for those campaigns. So we would see that, on average, if a campaign had perhaps one thousand dollars raised, if we put it through this amplification machine, logarithmically we could create a ten- or twenty- or one-hundred-times campaign, by getting it out there in the news media, on online channels, on social channels. Necessity is the mother of all invention; we had to invent a new way to create a mechanic that would help our marketplace grow.

Predicting the Next Earthquake

Tectonic plate shifts are hard to predict. But there are often early seismic signs before there are large changes in the movement of the Earth's crust. It's important to first remember that the backdrop to timing is identifying a small market (or niche) that is growing fast (or will grow fast). The reason is obvious. If you are too late, the opportunity is gone; too early, the opportunity may never materialize.

Of course, if I was super smart at this, I wouldn't have to write a book on it. I'd be living on my island off the coast of somewhere tropical, surrounded in a bunker by all my favorite things in the world. You know, like a James Bond villain.

This form of timing doesn't change often. If you are right, then you have a shot at riding an incredible amount of timing tailwinds. Think of Amazon or Shopify riding the huge wave of off-line to online shopping. You can also be wrong. Ask Facebook whether its big bet on Oculus was worth it. You have to argue that the year of VR has never arrived. But it probably looked like a reasonable bet at the time.

There are several different views on how to assess when a tectonic shift is going to happen. These tectonic shifts can be executed whether you are a small or a large firm. There are two variables to a timing shift: technology and behavior (or both).

Technology shifts: These apply some underlying technical innovation that doesn't necessarily require a behavior shift.

In many cases, the customers are already performing some task or function, and the technology shift just enables that function to be a lot more productive and/or adds a ton more in utility.

Here's an example of a technology shift: Zoom. For all intents and purposes, Microsoft should have owned digital video communications after their acquisition of Skype in May of 2011 for a whopping $8.5 billion. But Skype went through the post-acquisition doldrums and ceased to innovate. Zoom came along and developed an easier-to-use product with great audio quality. Their go-to-market plan and marketing were exceptional. Now Microsoft has basically killed Skype and is attempting to get market share back via Microsoft Teams.

Behavior shifts: These occur when customers decide to change their workflow or habits from one thing to another. These shifts are hard because you have to show tremendous value to the customer. Technology certainly plays some part in this timing element, but it's not the primary change. The change is that you are altering what a customer is used to doing. The quintessential examples of this are some of the most iconic consumer Internet businesses, like Uber and Airbnb. When these companies were young, you would have likely been unwilling to travel in a car outside of your traditional comfort zone of a taxi or a black-car service. Yet the value of convenience and certainty (you know where the car is) made Uber's utility so overwhelmingly compelling that the rest is history.

Another example: expense reports moving digital. I may be dating myself here, but I can remember when expense reports were a very manual process. Concur changed all of that. Their biggest competitor was paper, and they changed customers' workflow from paper to their digital solution.

The business was founded in 1993 and actually went through several near-death experiences through the Web 1.0 bubble crash. They also moved their business model from a perpetual software business to a SaaS business. The company was founded by three fantastic entrepreneurs: Steve Singh, Rajeev Singh, and Mike Hilton. Mike is one of the most sincere, smartest product executives and overall incredibly generous human beings I know. He is the rare executive who can seamlessly jump between wildly different business verticals and across any size of company. Here are his thoughts on taking advantage of these tectonic shifts:

How explicit was your strategic planning to capture the shift from paper to digital?

I guess in some ways you could say it was strategic. The context for the founding of Concur was the startup before it, which Steve Singh and I started together. Those were the early days of automating salespeople before Siebel, before Salesforce. We were literally automating people off Rolodexes. It's amazing to think my kids don't even know what those are.

But the founding of Concur was really about the idea of—let's find something else that everyone does that's completely manual, that software and automation and digital could have an impact on. Expense reporting was clearly one of those things. It had the appeal that literally everyone hated it. So there was tons of pain. Travelers, managers, finance, etc. There wasn't one part of that that was enjoyable or working. And it was all paper; it was literally paper. When we started Concur, 95 percent of all expense reports were done on paper. And the other 5 percent was like spreadsheets, mostly. And it was primitive, very primitive.

So we were strategic in looking at a paper process that we knew could be helped. We didn't totally know how software could fix it. And if you look at Concur's history, we started with shrink-wrapped software and ended up in the cloud and mobile. That was a long journey. We didn't totally know the "how," but we knew the "what." Like, it's going to be something about technology and software that could automate this. And the market was enormous. Anyone who travels or entertains has to fill out an expense report. So we knew the market was universal. In that sense, it was strategic. I don't think we totally knew how to solve the problem. But we knew the problem was solvable and was huge.

Did you pay attention to market timing, or did you have a hunch about the move from off-line to digital?

We were about having a hunch. The problem we were trying to solve had never been attempted this way—no one had tried to automate the problem, no one. It was literally 100 percent paper and manual. So if there was any sense of market timing for us, it was that the software revolution was on its way, personal computing was on its way. Going back to 1993, Windows 3.1 had cemented itself as the future of desktop. Personal computers had become ubiquitous in the workplace. So you knew that productivity was going to happen in some way, shape, or form, especially in the workplace. Everyone was going to have a PC, anyone white-collar, and if you think about business travelers, we had the hunch in 1993 that anyone who's traveling for business, the vast majority of those people have a computer. And so software was an opportunity. That was the idea on timing. The idea that here's a completely manual, painful process that can be solved with software. That was the hunch.

The market timing wasn't as much of a factor. We were going after sort of a greenfield opportunity. Our first product was literally shrink-wrapped software, and it was just for the traveler. We weren't even helping the finance department. Concur's first product was pretty fascinating. We had a sort of a QuickBooks-style interface. And we did all this insane stuff to print out an expense report that looked like your company's expense report. So the back end of the process was still paper. As far as the company was concerned, it was still paper. We were just automating the traveler. And we sold the shit out of that week. We were on the front page of the business section of the *Wall Street Journal*. Walt Mossberg [legendary tech writer for the *Wall Street Journal* and other mainstream publications] totally launched our company; it was a massive success, and we quickly, within six months, got out of the consumer business, because we knew we could have an interesting company. Intuit actually tried to buy us. We pivoted really fast to B2B, but it just goes to show, it wasn't about market timing. We had a hunch. And we tried something, and it worked. And we knew it wasn't the full answer, so we pivoted. We were a hunch company.

I think market timing is almost impossible. Hunches are way, way better. I think the odds of succeeding are way better with a hunch than trying to time the market.

This discussion reminds me of when Raj Singh [CEO of Accolade, co-founder of Concur] went to Silicon Valley several years ago and sat down with Ben Horowitz [co-founder and general partner at Andreessen Horowitz] and me. He told us something I'll never forget. He said, "In the modern world, if you want to start a company, you have to have a secret . . . something you know that no one else knows." That's kind of what a hunch is, in my mind. And he said [a secret is] "the thing you need," [as opposed to] anyone who thinks that they can just do something better than the way it is, but they don't really have a secret. "The cost of trying something is so low now." Of course, he's right. Somebody has more than likely already tried your idea. It's so cheap, with AWS [Amazon Web Services], and you can get an MVP [minimum viable product] up quickly. The cost of entry is so cheap; you really have to know a secret. What's your secret that you are basing your entire company on? That's all about a hunch.

When did you really understand that you had product/market fit at Concur?

Concur was a really interesting company. In one sense, we had product/market fit from the first day. If you can describe the problem you're trying to solve in one sentence or less, and everyone immediately understands, you're on to something. If it takes you a paragraph, and people are still kind of confused, you probably don't have the right idea. And so we had product/market fit in the sense that when you explain to a customer, "I'm going to make expense reporting automated and easy," everyone, from the very first day of that company to the end, immediately gets it.

However, the journey over twenty-plus years that we constantly had to reinvent was the "how." How do you do that? That side of the product/market fit is a constant process of reinvention. As new enablers came—the Internet, mobile, cloud, etc.—we had to reinvent the "how." That's a part of product/market fit. Also, we got into new markets. We started the opposite of Salesforce's customer target—we started up-market and moved down-market. That's a product/market fit problem. We went international. That's a product/market fit problem that took time, country by country.

So we had an awesome product/market fit from the very beginning; the "how" was constant evolution. It was hard, super hard. Even when we nailed the "how" in a market, the Internet came along. We had to reinvent everything when the cloud came. We bet the company on cloud. Mobile came along; we had to reinvent everything. So sometimes you can have product/market fit and things outside of your control come along, and you'd better rethink everything. I'm sure if you owned a taxi company fifteen years ago, you thought you had the ultimate product/market fit. What's more interesting to think about is that you can have product/market fit and then it can stop fitting really fast. What used to fit could not fit tomorrow.

What are some hacks that you have learned over the years that have helped you determine whether you are entering a market at the right time?

The obvious answer to me, where my brain immediately goes, is customer validation. I think there's a lot of tricks and muscle building for how to get early validation and how to approach it. When Raj Singh and I started Concur, he was like, twenty-five, and I was twenty-nine. We were kids. And one of the very first things we did was that we took a trip to the Midwest. We met a bunch of finance people: buyers, basically. And we literally drove around to like five people who Raj's dad knew. We just asked them a bunch of questions. And you know, back in 1993, that was a pretty good way to get some validation. That was a trick to basically figure out if the timing was right and if anybody would pay for the product.

In the modern world, it's a lot easier and a lot more sophisticated. But I think there's a definite skill in how you approach the market. How you test the market way before you launch anything, way before you build anything. I think those are essential skills. There's a whole spectrum there in the world of software and B2B software, which has been my world. There are hundreds of tricks inside of that, from the idea stage to a more developed idea across the value proposition, pricing, etc. There's a "maybe I'm even starting to build it stage," alpha, beta release; there's a whole spectrum of tricks where you can adjust or stop, reverse. I think that's an essential skill. It's a really good question. I'm not giving you a lot of specifics here, but I do think the answers are very complex and stage sensitive. If you're two guys in a garage who just have an idea, and you're starting out, that's one answer. There are hundreds of tricks.

Technology *and* behavior shifts: This is a great place to be. You are riding a change while customers adopt a new technology concept. An example of this is the move from PC to mobile gaming. Consumers were already playing games; they just were not doing so on their phones. The combination of taking advantage of smartphones—which added new computing power, graphics, and new capabilities—with consumers' existing hunger to play games, opened up a huge opportunity for aspiring companies.

I have a personal example from my days at GameHouse (a business unit of RealNetworks). I had a games business that was focused on PC gaming. We had some success in mobile gaming, but nothing like King or Rovio. In my role of running games at RealNetworks, I had a large network of game studios and development houses that we used to help us build our games. This included a mobile games studio partner in Finland. I will never forget the conversation I had one day with one of our "small" development houses. That company was Rovio. Of course, you know that name as the maker of the successful games franchise *Angry Birds*. I remember talking to Rovio's CEO, Mikael Hed. The conversation basically went like this:

> Me: Mikael, I hope you are well. I wanted to check in with you on how the relationship is going from your perspective.
>
> Him: [heavy Finnish accent] OK. However, I have bad news. We can no longer work with you.
>
> Me: Oh no, may I ask why?
>
> Him: Yes. We have just launched one of the most successful games and soon to be largest brands in the history of the world.

Rovio had just launched *Angry Birds*. I had a chance to catch up with Mikael's cousin, the co-founder of Rovio, Niklas Hed, in order to better understand the inside perspective on the timing related to launching one of the biggest video games of all time. Rovio made a big bet on a new platform, and it paid out for them immensely. They made a big strategic shift that was built on their insight into what customers wanted from their years of experience building games on traditional feature phones. Some fascinating insight from Niklas:

How did you know that the shift from PC to mobile was going to be the right driver for your business?

Actually, I didn't, at least in the beginning. I have to start from the beginning to explain. When I was a bit younger, I basically had two passions. The first was a nerd one. I have a programming background. I started programming when I was twelve years old, and my motivation for programming was gaming. I always had a dream that I wanted to work in the games industry when I grew up. My second heart was basically sports. I was swimming for the national team of Finland. I was seriously considering continuing down the swimming track as a focus.

But then eventually I went to university. I had a school project that was a programming task to make an interactive, multi-threaded, and over-the-Internet application. So that was the task, but I then quickly told my fellow students that we should build a game. It turned out to be a good game in the end, and that summer we entered a gaming event in Finland called Assembly. You basically compete with other teams. In that competition, there was a new category called "mobile games." We thought that it would be easy to take our game into mobile; it was a limited platform, and we thought that we could make a simple game that would work on that platform. The game was a real-time, multiplayer game. This was 2003, so the latency with the 1G network was awful. But we learned how to mask the performance issues, and we won the competition. Peter Vesterbacka [later chief marketing officer, aka Mighty Eagle, at Rovio] was running that competition for Nokia and HP.

As I thought about gaming, I was still at the university and I lived on campus. We all had crazy-fast Internet connections. We were basically streaming everything back in those pre-Spotify and -Netflix days. I knew that this was going to be the future. Everything was going to be streamed. Nothing was going to be local anymore. Even when I was building the game for the competition, I was playing an early version of the game at my parents' place, which is like an hour from Helsinki. It's in a place that is hilly, and cell signals were really bad. One day, I had a good signal, and I was playing our game on the front porch outside on a sunny day. I was playing it against my friend. That was the moment that I realized that streaming combined with Moore's Law applied to mobile devices—that was where the market was going. I was able to play completely wirelessly, anywhere and anytime. That was the point where I wanted to be in the mobile gaming business. There was going to be something new that would enable new applications and services. I knew that we were early with a multiplayer game, but my insight at that moment gave me the confidence to stay with the business.

Prior to the Apple iPhone and the App Store, most of your efforts [as a mobile gaming company] went into other things than creating the experience itself. I think a healthy ecosystem inevitably needs to be healthy for developers, and it also needs to be healthy for the end users. Having one phone, one standard screen size, a lot of memory, and a lot of processing power was like heaven for us.

But we actually didn't jump on the Apple App Store bandwagon immediately, because we were quite skeptical about Apple when they first launched the iPhone—even after they launched the App Store, which was a year or so after they launched the phone. In the beginning of 2009, we started realizing that this was actually the moment that we'd been waiting for, for all those years. Now the technical limitation and the distribution was being fixed, and that would also enable us to penetrate different markets through one point of contact.

We were in starving/hibernation mode prior to the iPhone. We used all the money that was invested into the company. When we realized that this was it, we started to worry that we were too late. There were a few games that were doing well, like *Doodle Jump*. We started making a few games for the Apple platform. *Angry Birds* wasn't the first one. We realized that although we were new to Apple, we were always a mobile-first company, and we had a lot of confidence. We knew what it took to make a mobile-first game versus the standard approach of "squeezing" a PC or console game into the mobile environment. Of course, not thinking mobile first is not optimal at all. We had the experience from working in the mobile environment for many years. By working with partners like Nokia, we understood how to do user research as well. All of those little things that we learned about mobile gaming compounded—we started to master mobile gaming over those years.

So, in terms of our success, we had the vision, and we were waiting for the right platform. Of course, you always tell yourself that there is no luck. But getting your own vision aligned with the [consumer demand] and getting the timing right— that is super hard.

What were the indicators and frameworks that you looked at to determine whether you were going to be successful in your social/mobile gaming pivot?

In 2003 the multiplayer game was the wrong timing. The tech wasn't there. The user experience wasn't there. The whole ecosystem wasn't there. We had the vision and insight, and we strongly felt that it was coming. As I mentioned, we were initially skeptical about Apple. But we analyzed what they were doing, especially their approach to distribution. The volumes were high; the business model was different. It was amazing. We knew their approach to the market was super smart and they were going to make it. They were going to set the standard. Those signs were clear to us. We then said to ourselves, "Damn, we better move and move fast."

Our vision was aligned with the underlying demand. We had *Angry Birds*, which was the execution of that vision. But it could have been that we would have developed another game. And I wouldn't be here. Gaming is a hit-driven business. At the time, we were even thinking about how to take the luck out of the equation. That was a common question between my cousin [Mikael Hed] and me.

We thought that if we could get enough parameters right for a new game on Apple with all our experience in gaming, that we had done our best and the rest was in the user's hands. If the user felt like the game was great, then we'd succeed. We knew mobile. We knew how to optimize the experience; we knew how to reduce load times, improve performance, and make a user experience that was smooth. We had the same mentality to user experience that Apple had. Because we'd been working with mobile for so many years, we knew that people were playing with "micro-pauses." Short game play. We knew that you had to build a game where the session could stop at any time without the user feeling like they were losing something. We also knew that users wanted instant satisfaction—a small dose of satisfaction, versus console or PC games.

What are some hacks that you have learned over the years that have helped you determine whether you are entering a market at the right time?

There were four things:

Customer-centric experience. On the phone, we knew that we were competing with other applications like the browser, email, and other games. We wanted our app to be the easiest choice to use on the iPhone. We spent a lot of time optimizing the load times. It doesn't seem that important, but it is. We knew from our experience that you had to be able to get an application running in the "magical six seconds." We had spent a lot of time in research labs [at Nokia], and we knew that we had to be able to start the game right away. We didn't want to have any kind of loading bars when moving around inside the game or anything. Everything should reside in memory. And it was a huge undertaking. Also, we optimized things like how many frames per second you should have. We decided that we wanted to be thirty frames per second; otherwise, the experience was bad. We also wanted our game physics to be universal. We wanted a game where you didn't have to explain the rules. We didn't have to have tutorials. We didn't have to have words. So the small things, which we learned from our years of experience, combined together made everything right for the customer for the mobile experience.

Treating our customers with incredible service. We realized that we could differentiate ourselves [in this new and massively growing market] by creating a service orientation to our games. These were the days of "premium games" [paying up-front to install a game]. We decided to update our game after a customer installed it, which was not obvious to do in the market at the time. Our thought was how we could delight users by serving new content [to existing players]. We speculated that perhaps we could boost the word-of-mouth activities around the game in order to drive more organic downloads. It worked. Users felt that we were serving them and that we were giving them this overwhelming value prop [for only a dollar]. We got super positive feedback from the end users. They thought we were great. We got consistent feedback that we were the best developer ever and that users were going to tell their friends. We then started climbing up the charts.

Also, we had a policy that if a customer sent us an email, we would respond to every single one. That was a huge differentiator for us because the big publishers never did this.

You couldn't reach out to them at all. You couldn't have an interaction. Our thought was different—if we want to create a brand, we want to be the good guys and build a close relationship with our customers. So we needed to play the game way differently. Rovio always liked to look at our weaknesses and turn them upside down. Rather, we challenged the dominant conventions and flipped those around to our own benefit.

Learn from your MVP (minimum viable product). When we launched *Angry Birds*, it was only on the iPhone. We had a lot of potential fans on Android. Android users *really* wanted our game. We gave these customers a future release date: summer of 2010. And the Android community was excited. But there were a lot of individual devices to support. It was hard to get that information on what devices were the most popular. We contacted Google. They said that we should just contact each hardware manufacturer. That would have been hard for us to do, and most companies would not disclose that information. So we were basically working blindfolded.

We then decided to take a negative thing and flip it around. So when we launched the game, we built a smaller version with only ten game levels. We added a button to report bugs, and when the user clicked on that button, it loaded a web page where we could read the device information. We were able to get all the specifications of all the devices (screen size, memory, etc.). We also could track the bugs reported by device. That helped us with our launch effort and to make the product better. And using that knowledge leads me to my next point:

Use your customers to grow demand. The bug-reporting page that I mentioned required the customer to enter their email information. We were able to collect 400,000 emails. Not only were we fixing bug problems on those platforms, but we were building positive customer sentiment. When we were ready to launch Android in a big way, I wrote a spam script. I had never written a spam script before. We were working with another launch partner, and then I sent the script to all the Android customers. The demand crashed the partners' servers continuously. We had, like, one million downloads in a very short time. But the server infrastructure wasn't that great, so it turned out to be a good PR stunt for us. Every time the servers crashed, we would use that as a PR stunt. That continued to snowball. More installs. More server crashes and more PR.

Finding Early Signals for Market Timing

As I have mentioned before, you have to solve the Goldilocks problem of not being too early or too late in a market. The key to timing a market shift is to suss out whether a shift is going to happen. This is one part intuition and one part data. In this section, I will first explore the core questions you should be asking yourself and then walk you through a set of data-validation techniques that can help give you some increased conviction on your market entry timing. The four core questions that you should be asking yourself are:

- Is there a large enough potential customer base for your new technology or service? (By the way, you can answer this first question from the work that you did in the first section.) Are you looking at a large base of customers that can have a large market value to you? Again, unless you are targeting a niche, you do not want to enter into a market where you and your firm garner just a small piece of market share that won't produce a potentially large business for you.

- Is the market that you're looking at full of competitors or not? The answer is going to be subjective, but you should be wary of seeing a lot of competitors with dominant market share in your addressable market. I would even say that if anyone is in the double-digit penetration, or there are several competitors in a market, you should flag this market as perhaps being close to being late. A folksy way to gauge this is if you already see competitor "roundup" reviews where editors are comparing and contrasting solutions. That—combined with someone who has a truly dominant share in engagement, consumers, or revenue share—should be a major red flag.

- Are the customers you're targeting underserved? This is another way to get at the competition for the service in terms of how expensive it is to acquire customers and whether customers find your propositions compelling.

- Is there some unique insight that tells you that the world is going to shift? This is *not* the insight about whether you have some interesting idea that only you think would be awesome. We've all heard those stories of a founder who believes in an innovation that they find compelling. What I am referring to is the insight that a market is going to change. Are there environmental, legal, macroeconomic, or other factors that are going to cause some form of market shift?

The last question is answered with what I would call intuition. With the first three questions, you can get reasonably close to identifying some early signals that I believe will produce measurable data on your market timing exercise. We will talk about these in the next section.

I have found that it's easy to convince yourself of whether a market is a real opportunity or not. You *can* apply the scientific method—really. I learned this when I spent some time at a startup studio in Seattle called Pioneer Square Labs. They are geniuses at spinning up an insane amount of ideas—and then killing a large number of these ideas. PSL has perfected what they call the Product Market Pull (PMP)—a series of techniques they have developed that embrace the scientific method to test whether an idea has merit. The number of agile processes they have developed is impressive. In general, you can get early signals that answer the core questions we just discussed by doing the following:

- Fake the product. Why spend the time building a product if no one is interested in the overall concept? There are many cheap and easy ways to determine if there's initial interest. One easy way, before you actually build out a product, is just buying ads. You can test your concept by creating a sales funnel with your product concept. You can test different value propositions. It's easy to set up an ad campaign on Facebook, Google, Instagram, etc. You can also deploy this strategy inside a product. You can build fake features inside an existing product (especially if your product is digital), things as simple as dialog boxes. You can even poll customers on how important they think the feature is. For example, my wife started a nonalcoholic beverage business called Rock Grace. She tested the concept of the product and perfected her brand before she had her product officially formulated. She started to acquire customers organically via Instagram and actually set up pre-orders of her product (which didn't yet exist), which helped her fund her product launch.

- Determine your customer acquisition costs. You can immediately learn how competitive the market for your potential idea is by buying ads that test your value proposition. You can drill into the specific customer segments very easily on Facebook as well. This enables you to find potential customers (who are potential customer interviews), and it helps you calculate how expensive it would be to acquire customers in your particular space. You can come up with hypothetical price points as well. An early flag is if there's already a lot of competition for your customers or if the cost of finding your customers is too high compared to the price point of your product or service. I tend to be very conservative when calculating my future lifetime value for a new product or service. I like to figure out if I can do better than break even on the customer's first purchase.

- Have a minimum viable product (MVP). We introduced this concept in the first section, and with *Angry Birds* on Android. The idea is that you build a version of your product that has the absolute scarcest features but can still be used by your earliest customers. This is a very agile concept that can be used quite effectively in digital products. You will want to make sure that you have built tracking and reporting into the product so that you can determine where your customers engage (or don't). Admittedly, there are some product concepts that cannot be MVPs. For instance, it would be difficult to build a minimum viable electronic car.

- Talk to customers. We have all heard of focus groups. It's easy to run a virtual focus group or connect with people in your network to discuss a potential idea. There are objective ways to set up these meetings, and I encourage you to

do your research on the best way to solicit potential customer feedback.

Here is a quick overview on some best practices from
Peter Denton, a growth marketer at PSL. Peter is a master
performance marketer who has used his unique approach to
determine which ideas at PSL's startup studio are worth venture investment.

**What are the key levers and frameworks that you deploy to deter-
mine if there's enough buyer interest in a new concept?**

At PSL, we have developed a methodology we call Product
Market Pull [PMP], where we try to identify signals from the
market before we invest significant resources in building out
an idea. This means that before we write a single line of code
or start designing mock-ups, we want to prove that the market
has real desire for the product or service we are envisioning.

In this process we start with customer segmentation and
really identify which specific companies and roles would benefit by becoming a customer. For example, if we are looking
to build a new technology that uses AI to improve account-
ing, we will create a matrix of customer segments like CPAs,
controllers, and CFOs across small, mid-size, and enterprise.
We then systematically test their resonance with this concept,
both through customer interviews and by running demand
generation to concept landing pages that outline the features
and core benefits to each customer segment.

In the end, we get really great signals, both qualitatively
through interviews and quantitatively through demand-gen
tests that show if and where there's pull in the market and
how strong that pull is. Since we've run these experiments
hundreds of times, we then have institutional knowledge

about the relative pull, and we can see when a market really wants a solution to a problem. The results can be compounding. Not only does the founding team know they are building a product that real companies want, but investors also gain conviction that they are funding something with real market potential. In the end, we are de-risking market mismatches through our own methodology, called PMP.

What are the specific tactics that you use to analyze your findings?

One thing that I love about the PMP process is that it not only informs you of the market's desire for your product or solution, but it also helps you understand your real TAM, SAM, and SOM [share of market]. Since we can analyze responses across roles, industries, and company size, we can really understand who is likely our initial market segment, how big that market is, and how hard it might be to go and win in that market. This really helps de-risk and add a lot of clarity around SAM and SOM. We can then extrapolate from their TAM and also understand where the gaps might be in the current solution to really achieve the full market potential.

This is really valuable because it provides a lot of focus for a small startup team. If you know out of the gate which market and persona you are most likely to win with, and how big that market actually is, you can really align your execution. Marketing can focus content and messaging on specific companies and roles, sales can predict realistic cycle times, and product managers can acutely focus on interviews with users that map to potential customers. Furthermore, since we run a lot of experiments in real distribution channels, we have some good initial insight into distribution economics, like how expensive it is to reach the target customer, how much it costs to get a lead, and which types of content resonate most strongly through PMP. This can be incredibly informative to a young team and save valuable time when entering a market and trying to figure it out as you go.

How important is finding the core customer segment in your analysis?

For us, it's critical and one of the main areas we focus on early. In early building we are very impacted by how scarce resources are in a young company, especially across product, engineering, and marketing. So having the ability to identify the core customer segment that is motivated for your product or service is so incredibly important. Not only does it provide clarity and focus to the team and investors, but it allows us to dig one level deeper in our initial GTM [go-to-market] on content, product level features, and value propositions specific to that customer set. For example, think about content alone. Producing good content is very cumbersome and expensive, likely requiring a few resources to craft a well-written, well-researched article. You then need a resource to distribute that content to a broad audience to try and see who across the market engages, adding more cost, and begin a customer nurture sequence that appeals to a broad set of customers. It can actually be a pretty risky gamble in the early stages to devote a lot of time and energy into something like this and have it not pay off.

Now, with PMP, where we can gain insight into market resonance before we go to market, we have an advantage. We can confidently focus our efforts into specific customer segments and content, reduce our ad spend to distribute to that audience, and craft nurture sequences that can be highly specific in the short term. For that reason, being able to identify the core customer segment becomes critical to our early research, knowing how large the returns can be for an early company.

How do you determine if the market is too crowded, from a competitive perspective?

One of the tactics we love to use in determining competition also comes from traditional digital marketing, specifically around keyword research in CPC [cost-per-click] campaigns. One of the benefits of letting advertisers compete against specific keywords is that they, by nature, define their competitiveness. For us, in the early stages of validation, this is an excellent way to see not only the true amount of competition in a space, but also the real potential costs to attract customers to that space.

Fortunately, products like Semrush make this process extremely accessible and efficient. In Semrush, you can put in a keyword or a competitor's web page, and Semrush will show you all the companies bidding on those same keywords. You will see not only keyword competition, but also overlap in bidding strategies, themes used in messaging, and their estimated spend to target customers across those categories.

This is extremely helpful for us. Once we know a few competitors in this space, we can use Semrush to see the entirety of companies competing and their estimated spend. This not only informs us of the true quantity of competitors and the value props they believe to be important to their customers, but also the amount of budget required to compete for early clicks. If the amount of competition is too high, and the budgets required to break through to new customers are upside down from the potential LTV [lifetime value], we know we have an issue from day one. There have been many times where this analysis has shown us that a market is too saturated and would be too expensive to compete in, and we ended up not building the business.

KEY TAKEAWAYS FROM THIS CHAPTER

Timing is the most difficult of the Insight Questions to answer. It takes both intuition and data to determine if you can time a market just right. Solving this Goldilocks problem of not being too late or too early to a market is going to take a keen perspective on the market that will be counter-intuitive to what everyone else is doing—and it will be scary for you as the leader, executive, and entrepreneur. If you're an early-stage business or a big business that's looking to pivot into an early-stage capital investment, you have to be aware of being too early. That's the single biggest thing to look out for.

I always like to say that making a few high-quality decisions on strategy is really what leadership is about. You will not be a market leader by counting on incrementalism. We all cannot be Steve Jobs, who had wicked intuition, but we can all be more thoughtful on how we can produce enough data to determine if a new business, product, or service has a stronger chance of success.

Here are some key highlights from this chapter:

- Market timing requires two things: identifying a small but growing market and identifying the likelihood of a technology or behavior shift in the market.

- Remember that finding a small and growing market is based on *your* definition. So when you look at an existing market and are trying to determine if there are too many incumbents, take another look at it from the perspective of whether or not there's a niche that you can exploit. Is there something in the market that you see could be an edge?

- You should answer the four key questions on market timing and then validate those with Product Market Pull data to validate your assumptions. Identifying the magnitude of the problem you're trying to solve by looking at customer acquisitions, the competitive landscape, and customer acceptance of your idea should make you more confident that you are not too early or too late to the market.

HOW WOULD YOU SCORE THIS SECTION?

It's time to score your second piece of the Insight Score. This question is about timing of market entry and whether the conditions are right for you to win, and it's one of the hardest questions to score. I would spend the time doing the real work on assessing your market timing. Do not rush when answering this question.

INSIGHT QUESTION #2
Timing. Are the dynamics of the market favorable to you?

How to score this question:

- It's unclear. (1 pt.)
- It's shifting in our favor. (2 pts.)
- Yup. It's good for us. (3 pts.)

On to the next question!

THREE

YOUR TRACK RECORD

INSIGHT QUESTION #3

Do you have a good
track record in this space?

3

SUPPLY CHAIN POSITION

Why Do Supply Chain Dynamics Matter?

It is vitally important to understand where you are situated in the supply chain. Those critical points of leverage are important so that you can anticipate how much control you have over your distribution. If you are not careful, you could cede your control to a publisher or aggregator. You must understand not only your current position in the supply chain but also where the potential pitfalls could be in the future. If you are a developer, an aggregator/marketplace, or a publisher, you need to understand how important you are to the source of supply.

The first step is to understand where you are in the pecking order. In the software business, you typically have a direct relationship with a customer. You're a publisher to an aggregator, or an aggregator to a customer. You can also be in both channels at the same time. First, let's define these roles:

Developer: This is the person or entity that owns the asset. The asset is anything that you have created. It can be an app, music, a book, etc. The developer can decide to distribute their content directly to a consumer or business by using their own distribution. For example, you could create a song, post it on your personal website, and charge for downloads.

Publisher: This is a company that typically doesn't create the asset for distribution but has some or all the ownership of the developer asset. For instance, in music, the music publisher owns the copyright, collects money (royalties), and oversees marketing, etc. You typically see this structure in media businesses when the developer needs distribution and money to help them create the asset. Examples in the music space are Sony BMG, Universal Music Group, etc.

Aggregator: You can call the aggregator the distributor. They own a platform that distributes assets. These assets can come directly from a developer or via a publisher. Aggregators can sometimes become developers as well. If you think about Netflix, they are an aggregator that is also a developer of their own content. Some examples of a distributor in music would be Apple Music and Spotify.

Entertainment companies like Netflix or HBO Max can have a direct relationship with customers. They also work with developers and may work with aggregators too. These can include classic traditional cinema theaters, which have historically had the first rights to show the movie because this "window" makes the entertainment company the most money (of course, this is starting to change due to online audiences and the pandemic).

Another example is gaming. The games business I once ran was both a publisher and an aggregator. We would own the rights to develop a game (splitting the economics with the developer) and publish the game on our platform. We also had a platform that distributed games that we didn't publish (or own the intellectual property).

Yet another example is e-commerce. Amazon is an aggregator. A large part of their business is selling third-party products, and they also distribute and own their own inventory.

The key is to understand the leverage. You never want to be seen with your proverbial pants down by losing control of your distribution. If you are not careful, you might end up ceding too much control on either side of the equation, whether to the developer, the publisher, or the aggregator. In the worst case, your business could be turned off. For example, Apple has turned off developers on their platform over a dispute, as we saw with the folks at Epic Games (the makers of *Fortnite*). Facebook has enabled certain developers to have unfettered access to their platform. At one point in time, the game developer Zynga had open access to all the users on Facebook—until Facebook closed that door to them.

The typical area to focus on, especially in the direct-to-consumer space today, is the relationship between a developer and an aggregator. You typically see a natural push-pull relationship between the two. Often the developer wants distribution, whether this is because they are a nascent developer, they are in a downturn (as happened in the early 2000s with hotel supply at Expedia), or they just want more surface area for their product or service. Aggregators typically start out as great platforms for distressed supply, breadth of supply, etc. They are always chippy about their long-term outlook. Since they do not actually own the supply (aggregating the developer's product), they know that their only role is to drive differentiated demand. Every aggregator knows that there is always a threat of developers bypassing them and going directly to a supplier. If an aggregator relies on a few suppliers (developers), then they are clearly in danger of not being differentiated.

For example, Netflix clearly understood this situation and was able to exploit the aggregator-to-developer role brilliantly. They started out simply distributing DVDs. No unique differentiation. The delivery method (by mail) combined with easy returns was a great business innovation for consumers. If you were ever hit by Blockbuster late fees, then you know that Netflix was a great flanker to Blockbuster. When they shifted to streaming, they were able to acquire streaming rights from the developers and focused on building their brand and audience sciences. They then invested in their own content programming so that they were not at the whim of the large media conglomerates (developers).

I will hammer this point home: you must understand where you are today and where you are going to be in the future in terms of your supply position in the market. Specifically, whether you are a developer, a publisher, or an aggregator, you will need to understand today's economics and where they will go in the future. Many of the world's best brands and companies that have been able to navigate this puzzle have taken their position as one of those supply players and strategically plot a course that has strengthened their hold on inventory. When you think of blue-chip companies like Netflix or Amazon, they were able to start out as aggregators and then develop size and scale to start to control their own supply. Whether this is making their own content, in terms of Netflix (in case they lose a popular movie or show), or in the case of Amazon, opening up their platform to third-party sellers and private labeling their own products, these large players understand that controlling supply is crucial to their long-term success. Another example: the Bellevue,

Washington-based game company Valve started out as a game developer and parlayed that position into a very successful game aggregator through their proprietary game platform, Steam. Valve doesn't rely on Apple for most of their revenues. They have built an ecosystem that they control.

Case Study: Expedia and the Dawn of Supply Market Making

Since we have been discussing the direct-to-consumer space, I wanted to tell a story from my own experience. This is not a story where I was the core leader and driver; I was merely a senior observer to what I call one of the most unsung battle victories in online travel. I like to think of it as a great Napoleon-like victory, like the Battle of Austerlitz. This was a win that not only secured an aggregator (Expedia) against developers (hotel suppliers) but also secured a key victory over another aggregator (Travelocity).

OK, let's dig into this example of how you should first determine your current supply position and economics. Since this was circa early 2000s, I am not revealing anything too proprietary. To set the stage, in around 2001 Expedia was an aggregator. They didn't own content (defined as an airline, car rental company, or hotel); they aggregated travel content. They were primarily an intermediary business that made money from suppliers, not customers. There were two sources of revenue: "rebates" from GDS (which we will define below) and hotel suppliers (aka commission).

Once you know what you are (developer, publisher, or aggregator), then the next step is to look at your unit economics. See the "sample" below (these numbers are way different now). The following chart shows the two models, before and after:

Unit Economics, Before and After (2002)

	BEFORE DOMINATION	AFTER DOMINATION
Revenue		
Customer Fees		
Air Commission		
Air Override		
Hotel Rev/Ticket	~$7	~$50 ← 7× revenue increase
Car, Other		
GDS Rebate		
Total Revenue		
COGS (cost of goods sold)	~$4	~$4
Contribution	~$25	~$70

Before I continue, I would like to explain some of the travel-specific jargon and acronyms. What is a GDS? A global distribution system or GDS is a central platform (typically run on old hardware platforms) that facilitates a transaction between a buyer and a seller. Sort of like a Visa or Mastercard for travel. Or in real estate terms, the multiple listing system (or MLS).

Traditionally, the buyer used a travel agent. Then intermediaries like Expedia and Booking.com became aggregators of GDS content. The value added for intermediaries (as seen by suppliers and buyers) was that they provided a better search experience (new search algorithms and platforms), better content (pictures, descriptions), and packaging (mixing and matching air, car, and hotel in consumer-friendly ways). It's also important to note that aggregators are always looking to bypass the GDS and have direct connections to suppliers. This happens today—some aggregators have even built a version of their own GDS platforms themselves. For instance, Airbnb created an entire platform for their own unique set of non-hotel inventory.

A GDS rebate was a revenue stream paid by the GDS to the aggregator. Each supplier (or developer, in our model) pays the GDS to include their content on the platform. Specifically, an airline, hotel, or car company puts their content in the GDS system for a fee, and the GDS then rebates a portion of the income stream to the travel agencies, intermediaries, etc., for using their platform. The more volume, the more of a rebate to the aggregator (like Expedia). All the other commissions flowed through the GDS to the aggregator. Again, the same principle applies—you can negotiate better commissions. This is before the airlines conspired against travel intermediators by creating a company called Orbitz, which was armed with a new type of price called the "Web Fare"—a story for a different day.

The rest of the commissions are paid by the supplier, whether it's air, hotel, or car. Not unlike most platforms, the aggregators receive more commission with increased volume. In this era, most of the money was being made by airline commissions, which on average paid about six dollars a ticket. All other providers, like car and hotel suppliers, were under a similar type of business model structure. However, the hotel piece becomes an important part of this case in controlling supply.

When I joined Expedia, the company was number two in its space against the then-formidable Travelocity. Travelocity offered the same content as Expedia since everyone was relying on the GDS content. But Expedia devised a plan to control more hotel inventory that was outside of the GDS (i.e., unavailable to travel agents), cheaper for consumers, *and* offered a higher margin to Expedia. This was a master stroke.

To explain, hotels are typically not booked first. When travelers start to book a trip, they think about their flight first, since that is the most important piece to start and end your trip. There are also limited airline competitors in each city you are flying into. Hotels, by contrast, have a lot of competition. Some are owned by larger conglomerates, and others are franchises of well-known brands. There are also many independent boutique hotels. The model Expedia invented (called the merchant model) was a key innovation that allowed them to establish both demand and supply control in the hotel marketplace. The company would secure bulk room rates from large hotel chains as well as independent hotels (like a wholesaler). These rates only existed in Expedia's databases—they weren't available to other travel companies or agencies, and they were initially available at significant discounts to consumers since they were sold as nonrefundable rooms.

Now look at the "after" side of the chart. You will notice that the margin jumps significantly. I mean significantly—almost three times the contribution per margin and over forty *incremental* margin dollars per transaction. That is extremely important. First, the inventory is differentiated. Expedia's merchant hotel inventory had some restrictions (e.g., it was nonrefundable), but the savings for a traveler were well worth the lack of standard flexibility. So customers saw better rates on Expedia than *anywhere* else online. Expedia could also control the sort order, meaning that there was marketplace competition between suppliers that Expedia controlled. This ensured competition, more market share, and even better rates.

Second, because of the margin expansion, there was a huge advantage for Expedia to acquire customers. Expedia was now able to acquire customers more efficiently, and they executed that effort like a well-coordinated WWII aerial attack. With the newfound margin, Travelocity started losing the war in buying advertising (primarily from Google) for an extremely long period of time. Their strategy was largely focused on selling flights rather than all the components of a trip. Expedia became number one and consigned Travelocity to also-ran, a status it never recovered from.

Now, over time this edge wore off. Travel suppliers started to get savvy and waged their own battles against the aggregators (like Expedia) with their own direct offers. They took control of their rates and offered price guarantees. The cycle continues to repeat itself. In fact, if you fast-forward to today's leading travel retailers, you can see that in terms of market capitalization, Expedia isn't the largest; Booking.com is much larger. They developed a business model innovation that was pulled out of Expedia's playbook. They built the ability to allow hotel suppliers to make their merchant hotels variable in margin, which was better for the supplier. When times were tight or fully occupied, the hotel suppliers had more control over their business, which helped Booking.com create more supply from the hotels. The cycle continues across every industry. You have to adapt your posture based on the market conditions and the competition.

This is the developer versus aggregator saga that we articulated earlier in this section, and it's always a challenge with an intermediary business. You must always have some unique edge for demand so that you can control your inventory classes (content, products, etc.). Competition among suppliers is always key! Building proper offensive strategies deeper in the supply stack can be a very promising strategy as well.

Case Study: When Your Software Has Zero Value Overnight

Supply dynamics typically do not get enough discussion. They are critical when you are looking for ways to unlock value in your business. Whether you are a developer, a publisher, or an aggregator, you need to be thinking ahead.

Today's battles of developers relying on aggregators is nothing new. For example, the Epic Games versus Apple lawsuit of August 2020 is a perfect example of a developer versus aggregator battle. Epic Games has disagreed with the role of app stores for quite a while. Specifically, they had an issue with Apple's restrictions in regard to their policies of charging 30 percent for application developers and restricting third-party payment and distributions outside of their app store. This tussle had *Fortnite* removed from the Apple App Store, which steamrolled into a very public legal battle (more on this below).

Again, as previously mentioned, you should be wary of building a business on a platform when that platform is extracting (or planning to extract) meaningful value from its developers. If a platform is extracting more value, then this is a warning flag to you as a developer. You will need to build additional distribution over time or secure specific protections via negotiated deal structures (e.g., most favored nation status) on that platform. But be nervous. Really nervous.

When I was a young product manager working for a company called WRQ in the early nineties, we had a PC-based TCP/IP software product line that basically disappeared. TCP/IP is the underlying communication protocol for the Internet. In the early days, you could actually make money selling a commercial version of it to enterprises. Back then, every large computer company had its own proprietary connectivity software. It's unbelievable for today's minds, but there were "giants" in mainframe and minicomputer computing that ran centralized hardware. I encourage you entrepreneurs out there to strive to build your business on your own terms.

Check this out. You had communication protocols like IBM's LU 6.2, a network protocol used for a type of network called Token Ring (versus Ethernet, the common networking framework used today). That protocol worked if you wanted to connect to IBM's big iron hardware, like 3260s and 5250s. Other vendors had their own solutions: HP with their HP 3000, and Digital Equipment Corporation (DEC) with their PDP and VAX lines of minicomputers. TCP/IP was becoming more popular as the Internet became more popular. Microsoft actually had their own proprietary protocol for Windows called NetBIOS. But the world was starting to change. Enterprises wanted more open systems that did not lock them into proprietary hardware and software. In fact, this battle between open and closed solutions continues today.

Back in the mid-nineties, Microsoft was on the verge of losing its edge with the Internet, which included its Internet browser. Then Bill Gates wrote a memo, called the "Internet Tidal Wave," that shook up his company and many of us in the industry. The date was May 26, 1995, and it was a call to arms for Microsoft to get serious about the Internet.

Microsoft did get serious. They incorporated capital and people, and they focused on putting the Internet at the cornerstone of everything they did. For WRQ this was trouble, because TCP/IP was suddenly part of the Windows operating system. I remember one of our product leaders gallantly trying to convince our larger-enterprise clients of the value of paid TCP/IP software. He authored a white paper called "TCP/IP: How Free Is Free?" Unfortunately for us, the answer was that free was pretty compelling.

Again, when you are building applications on someone else's turf, you do not have control. When that happens and the thing you have built as a developer is now an asset as part of that core platform and/or something they want to build themselves, then you are literally screwed.

Our revenues for that product line disappeared, and we eventually stopped selling it. As a young product manager, this early lesson in my first job in technology was a very good one that I have never forgotten.

Breaking Apart the Supply by Channel

So, think about trying it yourself. Start with what you are as a developer, publisher, aggregator, or some combination of the three. Then spend some time thinking through possible scenarios on how you see the future playing out. Is this easy? No. Can you be wrong? Most definitely. But you really want to be the most paranoid you can be when you do this analysis. Have a view and lock on it.

Here is a quick little template that you can use. You are first going to think through the outlook for each perspective and then think through the supplier's value proposition. You can start to capture some of those insights here:

Key Suppliers

CHANNEL	RELATIVE SIZE	COST OF DISTRIBUTION	FUTURE OUTLOOK	COMMENT
Developer	$xM in 2020	◑	Insert your info here	
Publisher	$xM in 2020	◑	Insert your info here	
Aggregator	$xM in 2020	◔	Insert your info here	

To break this down to make it more actionable, I typically look at the position I am in (developer, publisher, aggregator). Then I look at the relative size of each channel as part of my TAM or SAM. This can be difficult to figure out, but you can typically build a proxy for numbers that are directionally correct. Then calculate the cost in each channel from your perspective. For instance, Apple collects 30 percent from over $100 billion in applications in their ecosystem. The cost to the developer is 30 percent to the cost of goods sold. Apple has a much higher margin business with smaller hosting and fixed costs in terms of people and systems to run that business.

The overall category for gaming is in the trillions. There are different aggregators and direct strategies to deploy if you are a game developer. You have to decide the cost/benefit of many scenarios. You know that the supplier outlook is that Apple will likely not build their own games but will most likely build out a game subscription service (which they have already done). Apple has moved into developing their own content in other categories, like movies and music, so you should always assume that it's not off the table that they would become a competitor. However, you can start to build your own viewpoint and decide what future channels you will want to build to defend against any aggregation offensive. Each scenario is different. You will want to think very carefully and invite a lot of contrary thinking from your team and the industry to challenge your thinking.

Let's keep going with the game developer example. You should look at each channel (Apple, Google Play, your own direct channel, etc.) in terms of relative size as well as the cost of distribution. You're typically paying 30 percent to an app store. This is an aggregator-to-developer relationship. Some game developers publish third-party games that they do not own on aggregation sites. I did this back when I ran games at RealNetworks. Understanding the supplier cost of distribution is super important. It's also important to understand where your leverage is in the supply chain.

For instance, Epic Games, which (as I mentioned earlier) makes the epically popular game *Fortnite*, felt they could afford to bypass Apple's ecosystem. Apple has an offensive strategy (since they covet the 30 percent fee on their platform) and removed *Fortnite* from their platform. Many times, you see this develop when you have a strong brand bypassing a supply chain, feeling like it has the ability to pull margin back into the business because it's a branded experience that's unique. Epic thought they could bully Apple. At the time of this writing, the case is not yet settled, though I believe Epic will eventually prevail. Although the winds of US antitrust law are blowing very strongly against Big Tech, my guess is that Apple will have to acquiesce; the legal arguments on developer commission will be strong enough to sway the courts.

Spending time studying this relationship between where you are in the supply chain and how you are distributing your product is vital. Many of the most successful platforms allow software developers to thrive without the threat of competitive interference. In other words, the value capture of the developer exceeds the value of the platform. But that is not always the case...

The supplier outlook is super important. An aggregator one day can be a direct competitor to a developer tomorrow. You will typically see suppliers (developers) flex their muscles and continue to push their own direct-channel relationships with customers over time. This typically happens when a developer has had some level of success and believes they have enough demand for their product that they can start to make a play for a direct connection with a customer.

Not to belabor my point, but the dance between the owner of the content and the aggregator of the content is ever evolving and never static. Developers will always continue to push for direct channels to customers. The aggregator (platform), if not careful, will have more margin pressure over time. More direct competition then develops and threatens your operating margins. For example, it's not uncommon to see a developer compete with the aggregator for demand (e.g., buying keywords), which makes customer acquisition costs increase and leads to continued problems. The aggregator is not as competitive in driving unique demand to the developer's content, and, surprise, your platform becomes irrelevant over time. This happened to many of the competitive shopping engines that were once very dominant, like Shopzilla, Shopping.com, and PriceGrabber.com.

KEY TAKEAWAYS FROM THIS CHAPTER

You can unlock value by controlling supply, extracting more margin from supply, and offering a diversity of supply. This is critical as you assess whether you like your position.

Here are some key highlights from this chapter:

- Understand what your position in the distribution chain is today—are you a developer, a publisher, or an aggregator (or a combination of one or more of these categories)? This is key to better understanding your ability to control your own destiny.

- Plot a course. Think through where you are today and where you are going to be in the future in terms of your supply position in the market. Whether you are a developer, a publisher, or an aggregator, you will need to understand today's economics and where they will go in the future. Understanding supply is key to understanding where you have (or don't have) control over your own distribution.

- Always opt to develop a direct relationship with the consumer and to establish direct distribution as much as you can.

- If you are building a business on someone's platform (a developer relationship), understand the key motivators of that platform. Find out if the platform is seeking to extract more value from their platform. If yes, then start to plan your bypass or exit strategy.

- If you are an aggregator, understand how you can either build exclusive content for your platform and/or contractually lock up your supply. The natural instinct over time with developers will be to bypass your aggregation!

4

CUSTOMER VALUE ANALYSIS

You Like Me, You Really Like Me! You Like Me?

You must be really clear on what value you are delivering to your customers. *And* be clear how your customer value proposition maps to your strategy. This is a very important—if not the most important—thing to understand in Insight Question #3: Do you have a good track record in this space?

For early-stage companies, you commonly hear about product/market fit (PMF) analysis. Everyone has their own definition of product/market fit. There are many great books and thought leaders on this topic alone, and this section of the book will not try to give you a new definition. I am going to assume that you know what it is or can search for it via Google. My favorite description of PMF is from iconic investor Marc Andreessen, who has one of the most honest and visceral ways of describing it:

You can always feel when product/market fit isn't happening. The customers aren't quite getting value out of the product, word of mouth isn't spreading, usage isn't growing that fast, press reviews are kind of "blah," the sales cycle takes too long, and lots of deals never close. And you can always feel product/market fit when it's happening. The customers are buying the product just as fast as you can make it—or usage is growing just as fast as you can add more servers. Money from customers is piling up in your company checking account. You're hiring sales and customer support staff as fast as you can. Reporters are calling because they've heard about your hot new thing and they want to talk to you about it. You start getting entrepreneur of the year awards from Harvard Business School. Investment bankers are staking out your house. You could eat free for a year at Buck's.

Or as I like to say, everything just sort of works without a lot of effort.

I personally like frameworks to make decisions. This book has a lot of frameworks. If you want a good working version of PMF, I love the Silicon Valley mojo (by saying "mojo," I am already not that cool) of Rahul Vohra, the founder and CEO of Superhuman. He is prolific in his content marketing on common-sense business frameworks, especially around designing and launching products. He has popularized the "product/market fit engine," which is a simple equation to determine if you have product/market fit. The formula is simple: when over 40 percent of users would be very disappointed without your product, then you have product/market fit. Rahul sends out a survey, asks the questions, segments the data based on who says they would be disappointed, then builds a product for that audience after probing them a bit more. Then he continues to iterate to increase that percentage of disappointed users, and voilà, he has built a very targeted product experience for a very targeted audience.

I will stand on the shoulders of giants on PMF. It's certainly an early signal for an early-stage company. The product should be the most important thing you're offering customers. You should know your pricing, packaging, and positioning. But if you're reading this book and you already have an established product and are now trying to jump a couple of squares to be a market leader, you also need to be able to dissect your position in the marketplace. This is beyond the product; it's taking a step back and looking at the chessboard. You really need to understand your position in terms of the strategic value that your product serves its customers.

Pick One: Low-Cost Strategy or Premium?

Let's back up to the earlier example of Michael Porter and the point about a low-cost or differentiated strategy. One of the analyses we used back in the day to identify the value that was being provided to customers was to plot the "perceived price" and the "perceived benefit." You can collect this information easily from a five-to-ten-question, statistically significant survey. I have also found that you already know in your gut how your product will be mapped regardless. I like to do this to include any segments (firmographic, audience type, etc.). For instance, if you are selling a productivity sales ops tool to different verticals and company sizes, they are probably going to compare your product or service differently. I also like to use this same graph to plot my competitors. What you want to see is that you are creating a value advantage. Remember, this is typically low-cost, no-cost, or premium.

This exercise is strictly used to evaluate how the consumer is perceiving your value proposition. It's not a competitive analysis exercise. Those exercises typically involve a breakdown of the specific features and functionality of your product versus your competitors'. You know what I am talking about—one of those charts with Harvey Balls (balls with zero to full circles filled in based on the completeness of an offering). That is an exercise for a product manager.

Value is different—it's not the actual feature; it's the perception of the offering as a whole. Companies get this wrong all the time by building products with feature after feature. The best companies decide on how to build a product to a specific set of segments and build a brand to reinforce that proposition. The packaging and pricing are simply an exercise after you have done this work. We will cover this topic later in the book, but do not think about value as anything more than the perception the customer has about your product or service.

Back to it. Look at the chart on page 105. Do your plotting. You can be as quantitative and as qualitative as you like. Again, you can get a sense of where you are on the value spectrum from focus groups and quantitative market research. You should also take a look at your win and loss data to help you pull out some customer verbatims (aka open-ended comments in surveys) and insights.

Plot Your Customer Segment Value

First, start to plot your current value advantage against each segment. The key thing to focus on is whether you have a segment (e.g., mid-market versus corporate accounts) where you have more advantage. Hopefully you do not find yourself in a position where you don't have a value advantage in any segments. For extra credit, you can also change the size of the bubble to represent a financial metric or a percentage change in the market segment growth.

You might think that I am a consultant, but I am certainly not. I am not even an MBA. But I sure like my two-by-two (2×2) charts. Earlier in my career, I had a habit of screwing with my fellow product managers, who were your typical Stanford and Harvard types, by hiding the markers as they were about to draw their own two-by-twos. Ah, the profanity and the loud exclamations of disbelief could be heard for miles. They couldn't run a meeting without a marker. Checkmate!

When you look at your perception plot based on your own offering, you should be as quantitative as possible. For B2B, you can acquire data on verticals relatively easily through publicly available data. For example, you can get Standard Industrial Classification (SIC) codes quite easily. For consumer businesses, you can also get data on demographics and psychographics. Get creative. You can get a lot of free data from sources like App Annie, Facebook (e.g., "Info and Ads" to literally see all the ads that your competitors are testing in one place), Semrush, and other ad tools. You want to make sure that you have the best data to ensure that you can tease out where your product fits in relation to the type of customer you are trying to serve.

Case Study: B2B Example of Too Many Segments

Here is an example of a plot from a former company, an HR tech company. The firmographic is detailed below. The bubbles were plotted qualitatively based on sales churn data—in other words, why a customer churned. In this case, the desires of the business did not necessarily scale to the desires of the segment. This is a typical issue with companies both big and small. They want to build something that is everything to everyone. You can do that when you have significant size and scale, but it's very difficult when you are an early-stage firm or one trying to pivot into another segment if you are part of a larger firm.

When you do this exercise, be sure *not* to believe your own bullshit. Looking at a chart like this would flag that large companies see the most advantage, but your perceived price is too high. Digging into this some more, you would have found some very specific red flags, primarily around the product not being able to scale from its current segment (small companies) from a data- and change-management perspective. In fact, the amount of data and exposure to employee data was very hard to manage for big companies. So be careful not to convince yourself that your view of the customer value proposition and distinctiveness is the same as your customer's view.

Trying to be all things to all segments at the same time is a recipe for disaster. A point that I will reiterate over and over again is that you must be willing to pick a point of entry. You will not find, for instance, many B2B companies that started out targeting small, medium, large, *and* F500 companies. When you plot your segments, make sure they're backed by data.

When you see instances where your perceived price is high and your benefits are high, don't run away. Look to see if there's competition in that segment that is offering the same or a better solution at a more attractive price. Obviously, you want to be in the value-creation side of this diagram. You can make any argument you'd like when you are plotting this customer value analysis, but you will also need to be aware of the competitive value plot, which we will talk about next.

Plotting your customers' perception of your offering is a very good checksum on your operating hypothesis. Arm

Customer Value Analysis

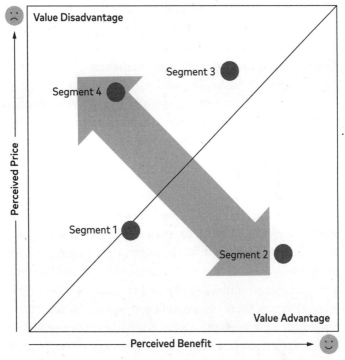

yourself with enough data to be clear, and insist that you have investors, board members, and your team in the intellectual Thunderdome (this is a reference to the 1985 postapocalyptic action movie *Mad Max beyond Thunderdome*) with you as you do this exercise. And be wary of an analysis that says that you are attractive to multiple customer segments equally.

Plot Your Value Compared to the Competition

Mapping your value compared to the competition is another interesting way to check your assumptions about how your customers perceive your product. Competition is a validation that you have a compelling product and service that customers want. But it's easy to get too focused on your competitive moves. However, understanding a competitor's strategy is super helpful, as it helps to reinforce where you can apply product, pricing, packaging, and positioning strategies. The example below shows this, and it also reinforces the earlier discussions on picking either a low-cost distribution strategy or a premium strategy. Chapter 5 will also guide you in terms of competitive analysis.

Before you start to map your competition, please do not ask your customers directly about your price point. They won't give you an honest answer. They won't want to offend you by saying your product or service is too expensive, so they won't be open and truthful. I prefer to use questions (like using a Likert scale) that tease out the answer. For example, ask the customer if they have looked at competitive solutions. If they say yes, then ask a conditional question like, "With regard to the competitors you looked at, how would you compare <your solution here> to the pricing offered by the competition?" There are a ton of free question banks that can help you tease out the relative pricing advantage and relative value advantage. Keep the survey short and concise.

These types of charts are very clarifying for you, your team, your investors, and your board. Typically, you see an endless array of PowerPoint slides with reams of data. Why not nail your perspective in one slide? At the very least, you should be asking yourself if you are appropriately positioned against other competitive alternatives.

Again, this is not a feature stack rank exercise (tech product manager speak for a priority list of features by importance). This is the perception of value and price. You can do this in many different ways. Personally, the quickest way for me to want to jump out of a window is when I hear someone on my team ponder how they would get this insight: talk to customers, send a survey, etc. This should not be hard to figure out and should not take more than a couple of days. No large expensive market research is required.

Case Study: Rosetta Stone Goes Premium

Here's another recent example from Rosetta Stone. As I previously mentioned, when I started at the company, the focus was on a smaller SAM: the enterprise language-learning market. Before I even got to the customer value proposition phase covered in this chapter, it was very clear to me that we needed to pursue a larger SAM as part of the language-learning market, where we had a competitive advantage: the US consumer language-learning market. It was also easy to get a read on this decision since Rosetta Stone was a twenty-seven-year-old company. We had customers and products in the market. The competitors in the space were easy to talk to as well, so it was easy to dissect their traction as well as their strategies. Getting a sense of the relative perception from customers was simple too—we could survey them and actually talk to them. You may not have this luxury when you are trying to pivot into another segment or market. However, I would highly recommend spending literal face time with your customers. Just because you are an executive does not give you an excuse to outsource your customer empathy.

Earlier in the book, I discussed the US language-learning market. Rosetta Stone was focused on a geography strategy (most of our sales were in the US) because our brand had the largest market share in terms of brand awareness. Our focus was to lean into the premium differentiated strategy since that reflected our brand promise. We decided to also price and package our product as a lifetime unlimited bundle. We did lots of testing on pricing and packaging options and decided to load more and more value at the highest LTV (lifetime value) at scale, which worked.

When you lean into your strategy, everything makes more sense, from your product to your pricing. We leaned in heavily on our lifetime unlimited pricing, meaning that you could pay one price for unlimited access to over twenty-four languages. We did that to establish the highest LTV in the competitive set but also because we wanted to acquire customers who were clearly in our target at scale. We then continued to add premium features that bolstered this SKU as support for our premium and effective positions. For instance, the "unlimited" languages feature had high resonance with our customers, so we then continued to add more capabilities that didn't add marginal incremental cost but bolstered our intrinsic value.

However, one aspect of this analysis that we highlighted was that our competition was scaling revenues faster than we were. The core reason why we couldn't keep up was that we were a public company that was capital constrained. The competition started to spend a lot of money on customer acquisition. This was but one of many factors that helped us rationalize taking Rosetta Stone private in 2020. Best brand, great product, highest LTV—but without the proper capital to scale at our opportunity level.

KEY TAKEAWAYS FROM THIS CHAPTER

My high school track coach, Pat Tyson, who is still a tremendous mentor for me, used to always say two things about the competition: "If you look behind you, versus looking forward, you will lose time expending effort," and "Never let the competitor get farther than twenty feet ahead of you—there's an invisible umbilical cord between them and your will. Let that person get too far out ahead, and your will is going to snap." That's how I think about competition.

Here are some key highlights from this chapter:

- Taking an honest and data-driven perspective on your customer value proposition is key to determining whether your product is aligned to where your segmentation is creating value and your competitive value proposition.

- Low-cost or premium differentiated? Pick one of those strategies and lean into it. Do not try to be a "tweener." It will be too easy for another player to either lean into value per transaction or price per transaction.

- Map your current customer value proposition by segment using data or qualitative means. This enables you to identify areas of white space (areas you can take advantage of), segments or problem areas, or even areas of focus.

- Additionally, map your competitive value proposition. Layer in growth rates as well, to better understand your value advantage versus the competition. If you don't have a good product proposition, you are in real trouble.

5

THE COMPETITION
YOU VERSUS THEM

As a product manager, you act like an overprotective parent. You fawn over that child (the product) and make sure that nothing bad happens to it. As a recovering product manager, I find that competitive analysis is one of my favorite things. I love the feeling of getting those competitive juices flowing.

This section is *not* competitive analysis on your product or service. This is competitive advantage analysis between your company and the companies you compete with, directly or indirectly. It's a critical part of dissecting the relative performance of your business. It involves several steps. At a high level, these are:

- Relative performance: What is the size and scale of the businesses you are competing with? This involves looking at bookings and EBITDA (earnings before interest, taxes, depreciation, and amortization).

- Determine your business advantage versus the competition: List out where you are and are not advantaged. Summarize your overall advantage.

Why is this important? It will help you do the following:

Assess a weakness. Amazon CEO Jeff Bezos is famous for stating that "your margin is my opportunity." Understanding how a competitor makes money can be an avenue for an attack, especially when you are competing with an eight-hundred-pound gorilla. Larger companies often protect their existing business because the pain required to change that business (or business model) is too great.

Determine the capital structure. Understanding what advantages a competitor has, whether it's cash or currency (stock liquidity), is super important. The most important accelerant to growing your business is your ability to deploy capital. If you are up against a formidable competitor that can outspend you, think very carefully about how to engage in battle.

Relative Performance

This is easy to figure out. Depending on whether the competitor is public or private, you have a huge array of resources to pull from. For example, for private company data, PitchBook; for app and website traffic, Semrush and Moz; and for private filings, some countries actually make them publicly available.

Call them: yes, talk to competitors. You will be surprised how many will both take a meeting with you and tell you some interesting tidbits about their business.

There are a ton of further examples. The point is that there's no excuse for not knowing. Here are some additional ideas for you:

- Hire a former executive from your top competitor—after first making absolutely sure that you are not violating any terms of a nondisclosure. I have seen this work really well in the past. Even an executive that is adjacent to your space can provide some useful context on your competitors.

- Have a bear versus bull session. Make this a team exercise on how one or more of your competitors could kill you. Make it fun. Hand out prizes to the best team. Make it feel like Model UN from high school. You will be surprised what insights you unlock while running this friendly competition.

- Put a target on your competitor—not literally. I will never forget former CEO of Expedia Rich Barton driving this home to the entire company (pun intended). At one meeting he showed a picture of a car's tail lights with Travelocity's logo as the license plate. We knew everything about Travelocity. When we beat them as the number-one seller of travel online, he then showed the same image with the American Express logo in the license plate. "Our goal is now to be the largest seller of travel in the world." What is your culture's way of focusing on someone or an idea to go after? It can really drive action and focus.

This type of motivation is electrifying. It emboldens you and focuses you. If you can steer your company toward a goal larger than yourself, then amazing things can happen. For me, the intrinsic motivator was never bragging about a victory over someone or something else; it was always about the satisfaction of achieving something greater than I ever thought possible. Or as my track coach Pat Tyson would always say, "That person in front of you wants it more than you do." Putting a competitor that is larger than you in your crosshairs is a great way to get organizational clarity and focus.

Advantage versus Us

This seems obvious: Just list the strengths of your competitor alongside your strengths. While you do it, look to fill in the following:

- Capital war chest.

- Key competitive advantages in product.

- Number of customers.

- Unit economics analysis (LTV, CAC (customer acquisition cost), renewal, retention rate).

- Scale advantage: ability to amortize costs across their business.

- Size advantage: the size of the army (e.g., huge sales team).

When you can get more detailed data, you really start to understand everything about a competitor. It becomes visceral, and it becomes personal. Here is a vivid example. If you have never watched the movie *Hoosiers*, starring Gene Hackman, I would highly recommend it. There's a pivotal scene during a playoff game where the coach (played by Hackman) tells one of the players, Buddy, to stick "like gum" to his man on defense. The exchange is wonderful. He advises Buddy, "By the end of the game, I want to know what flavor he is." When Buddy later fouls out of the game, he tells the coach, "He was Dentyne."

Case Study: RealNetworks Poked the Bear

Here's an example from my past, when I was product manager of RealPlayer in the early '90s. At that time, RealPlayer was the most successful streaming product on the market. It enabled anyone to listen to audio and video over the Internet. Yes, RealNetworks invented streaming. The company was a high-flying Wall Street darling with lots of confidence and moxie. But it flew a bit too close to the sun when it decided to initiate a full-frontal attack on Microsoft.

I will indulge you with a bit of the background to show you why you can have a very bad future when you don't understand your performance and capabilities against an eight-hundred-pound gorilla intent on wiping you off the board.

Back in the early '90s, Microsoft was dead set on not losing its advantage in the marketplace. As previously discussed, the company had already completely changed their strategy to incorporate the Internet into everything they were doing. At this point in the story, Microsoft was making steady progress in the browser wars, gaining ground on Netscape, the market leader. Microsoft was rapidly improving its browser, Internet Explorer, which was offered free as part of the Microsoft Windows operating system.

It was clear that Microsoft was going to continue to dominate the Internet. They were incorporating more and more functionality inside their platform for free. Of course, this is not an uncommon tactic for Microsoft and many other platform companies. In fact, it still happens today—look at what they are doing with Microsoft Teams by including it for free in their offerings to diminish Slack's (or Zoom's) market dominance. When we discussed platforms in Chapter 3, we said that if a platform wants a capability and you rely on that platform, then they will either brute-force replicate that capability and/or threaten to buy you out. It's part of the developer versus aggregator saga.

Back to the story. Microsoft was getting more serious about building their own streaming service, called Windows Media.

They were incorporating this capability for free in their server software. They didn't need to make money on streaming; they just wanted more licenses of their server and client software. But RealNetworks made its money from selling streaming media servers. The software was sold on a per-stream basis, meaning that if you wanted to have larger simultaneous audiences, you would have to pay more money. It's funny to think about that business model in today's pervasive streaming media world. Early adopters were media companies. Business was good, and RealNetworks went public and had a giant market cap. But Microsoft didn't have to make money on streaming; they could incorporate this capability and use their existing software business to fund this incremental capability.

Without getting into too much detail, RealNetworks and Microsoft decided to be "frenemies." RealNetworks licensed Microsoft the source code to the RealNetworks technology. Unbeknownst to Microsoft, RealNetworks was very wily and only licensed a specific version of the source code. RealNetworks then upgraded the protocol, rendering all improvements (not available to Microsoft) to be obsolete. Microsoft thought they were buying the ability to have ongoing capability improvements—one Microsoft product to stream all formats. To be clear, there was no malfeasance or any action that violated any legal agreement. However, the spirit of the relationship was certainly broken, which started this major market battle.

As you can imagine, this upset Microsoft. RealNetworks poked the bear, and what happened next was similar to what befell Leonidas of Sparta—a small company against the might of the Persian army. There was eventually a large settlement that benefitted RealNetworks, but the damage was done; RealNetworks lost the streaming wars and ended up a shadow of its former self.

When you step back and apply this story to studying competitive advantage, you will quickly be able to identify the following: Microsoft had the ability to fund the inclusion of streaming software. RealNetworks was reliant on servers for their business model. The loss of content in the RealNetworks format meant less content to watch, which then meant that there was a smaller audience downloading the RealPlayer, so the media format became less popular.

RealNetworks didn't have the capital or the leverage to take on Microsoft. But they still decided to play hardball by inciting the wrath of one of the biggest industry titans. Microsoft accelerated the bundling of its streaming service and put its considerably larger teams to work attacking RealNetworks. Overnight, it felt like there was an army of product managers, developers, and executives focused on eliminating RealNetworks. The battle could have been delayed. RealNetworks eventually won the lawsuit and was awarded a huge settlement, but at what cost? RealNetworks today is a footnote of its once mighty self. There was no Plan B. The company moved into a variety of different business models after the Microsoft settlement but never again scaled the heights it had once dominated.

It's always easier to play armchair quarterback in hindsight. But when you think about the meta, you can identify the moves that a large incumbent will make when threatened by an upstart. Microsoft was already well through diminishing Netscape's market share. I shared an earlier example of how they eliminated a TCP/IP product that was bundled in the operating system. The advantage was there (via the operating system bundle and their massive market dominance). It's hard to avoid an avalanche.

The key to this analysis is understanding, with eyes wide open, the constant forces around the industry with new and existing players. Hopefully you can see through a plan to build a significant compared advantage that you can defend against large players.

To get a more expert-based/practitioner perspective, I asked product management executive and influencer Soumeya Benghanem to articulate her perspective on her best practices on competitive frameworks:

How do you think about the competition overall?

First, let's talk about the definition of competition. *Merriam-Webster* defines competition as either "the effort of two or more parties acting independently to secure the business of a third party by offering the most favorable terms" or "active demand by two or more organisms or kinds of organisms for some environmental resource in short supply." While these hold true, when I evaluate who the competitors are for my business or product, I take it a little deeper to make it actionable. I also look at what companies or products are looking to compete for my specific target customers' money (share of wallet) and what other products my customers will put in their frame of reference for that purchase decision (context is king).

Porter's Five Forces and SWOT [Strengths, Weaknesses, Opportunities, Threats] are the two frameworks I have used in most of my work. Over time, the resulting tables of data and presentations that contain the competitive information become complex artifacts that require an analyst or PM [product manager] to spend what amounts to a few months every year keeping them up to date.

It's extremely important to garner a deep understanding of several things my competition is doing, including their product, new segments, customer affinity, usage, where they might become new entrants, etc. While this knowledge is imperative to use as one input into my strategy, it's not the primary input for my product road map, backlog, or strategy. Many businesses are too reactive to competition and lose sight of their own vision and unique value proposition. Said another way, it's impossible to differentiate if we do not have a broader understanding of the offerings in the market, and it's difficult to prioritize without knowing the potential outside threats to our business. This understanding enables us to clearly define our potential customer segments' pain points so we can identify an unmet need and deliver against that problem or provide a better solution than exists today.

When I led product at Remedy Health Media, we found ourselves in an extremely competitive category with very thin margins and were competing largely on keyword and search engine arbitrage to drive traffic to content. That's a reality of ad-supported revenue models in a highly saturated industry where anyone with a blog or an Instagram account is a competitor. We could not win by competing on arbitrage in the long term. It's a great example of where we needed to worry less about what the competition was doing, and instead step back and create a new product that had a unique value proposition.

Even when you have differentiated yourself, it's critical to also understand where the gaps are in your strategy, customer experience, and product (yes, we all have them). The gaps we create provide the opportunity for new entrants to come in and potentially disrupt our business. A famous example of this was when in 2008, Jim Keyes, the CEO of Blockbuster, told a journalist, "Neither Redbox nor Netflix are even on the radar screen in terms of competition." Both of these companies were able to come in and reinvent the entire category and make Blockbuster obsolete. One of the important reasons was that customers *hated* late fees, and that translated into customers really disliking the experience and customer service.

If Blockbuster was more focused on customer insights that take precedence over competitive analysis, and on the gaps in their own value proposition as well as the overall technology trends, they would have been able to reinvent their own business model before others closed that gap.

It's equally important to watch both overall trends and what other companies in other segments are doing to define your road map. I often find inspiration in completely different businesses, in both their approach to customer needs and reinventing business models. Pairing this knowledge with my deep customer insights and an intimate understanding of what our business and team can do better than anyone else helps me create a road map that stays ahead of the competition. Ultimately, the customer is going to define what we do.

Many leaders spend too much time really worried about their competitors, and some even make negative or comparison statements about them to their own team, investors, and even customers. In most cases, this is counterproductive and damaging. In fact, competition can be a *really* good thing. Competition can prove there is a market need. Competition can bring bigger awareness to a new category. Competition can help create a market where the total market size and demand are much larger than one company alone could create. Competition can set pricing at higher levels. Competition can help emphasize where you are different.

At the end of the day, it's critical to know who your customer is, what they do well and not as well, and where they can possibly expand, in order for you as the leader to better interpret customer insights, develop your unique value proposition to deliver on *your* vision, minimize risk, delight your customers, optimize your solution, maximize your credibility, and win.

KEY TAKEAWAYS FROM THIS CHAPTER

While I have said previously that you should not be overly obsessed by competitors, you should understand the relative competitive advantage. How else are you going to decide if you are going to be able to be successful in a new market or moving into an adjacent market?

Here are some key highlights from this chapter:

- Make competitive analysis a team sport. Get your team involved, make it part of your strategic planning, and have fun with it. Know your competitors like you know your favorite sports team.

- Do your homework. Collect and retain a library of competitive data so that you can start to build out a view as to your competitors' business moves. Capital structure, key hires, etc., are important signals for you to track. At some point, you will more than likely need to raise capital. Understanding your competitors' strengths and weaknesses can provide clues as to when you need to do this.

- Understand the chinks in the armor. Make sure to understand what your competitors are good at by assessing their relative performance as well as how you are advantaged (or not).

HOW WOULD YOU SCORE THIS SECTION?

It's time to score your third question. This is the scoring on "Track Record." You'll know if you have product/market fit. You'll have a good sense of your momentum getting customers, working with suppliers, beating the competition, etc. Your track record doesn't have to be strong in order for you to have the ability to jump into a new market position. But it can certainly help.

INSIGHT QUESTION #3
Do you have a good track record in this space?

How to score this question:

- It's slow going—too soon to tell. (1 pt.)
- We have a strong fit. (2 pts.)
- We have an advantage. (3 pts.)

On to the next question!

FOUR

PLANNING

INSIGHT QUESTION #4

Do you have an executable plan?

6

IDENTIFY YOUR STRATEGIC OPTIONS

WAS A HUGE fan of *The A-Team* in the '80s. It was your typical popcorn-style action show that was light on plot depth but heavy on action. The premise for the show involved four members of a former military unit that acted as guardian angel–style mercenaries. Their wily leader was played by George Peppard. His character, Colonel John "Hannibal" Smith, always found a way to lead the team through any situation. His catchphrase was, "I love it when a plan comes together." I personally always prided myself on having a Plan A, a Plan B, and of course a Plan C. Perhaps good old Hannibal Smith was an early influence.

If you are feeling good about everything leading up to this question, now is the time to define your plan of attack. Think through where you are applying your energy, capital, and focus based on your unique advantages. By now you have walked through the first three Insight Questions in this book, so figuring out your plan of attack should be fairly simple.

Well, it *should* be. If you are in the right market, with the right timing and some traction, you may be off to the races. The wind is at your back. However, from personal experience, I have seen businesses in this position blow it because they didn't focus their time and capital on the right initiatives. Even if you have a great business that's growing in a market that is exciting and lucrative, sometimes you stumble because you don't earmark the appropriate amount of capital resources on a particular plan.

Every business comes down to controlling four operating dials (more on these below). Each one needs a certain amount of resources and prioritization. In some businesses you'll need to use some dials rather than others. For example, in a marketplace company you will need to figure out what portion of your business is focused on acquiring supply (customers that are paying you for completed sales, leads, or whatever) versus the demand side of the equation (you driving business to your customers). Other businesses might need to focus on a completely different set of initiatives. We will walk through some of the common areas below.

Reviewing Your Operating "Dials"

I often find that businesses sometimes aren't explicit about their focus and don't coordinate their plans across the company. A common problem is what I call "spraying and praying," meaning that you are trying to do too much, and so you are not doing very much well. You may be able to hide this issue during the good times, but the bad times tend to reveal it. I always recall the quote from legendary investor Warren Buffett, who said, "Only when the tide goes out do you discover who's been swimming naked." When your business hits an operating snag, whether it's slowing sales or capital constraints, you will quickly figure out if you have over-allocated your efforts. If you look down and don't see any clothes, you'll know you've been caught out.

The four dials that I like to look at are:

- Selling more to the same customer (via cross-sell and upsell).
- Selling to new customers.
- Increasing demand.
- Just buying it (inorganic).

Operating Dials

| Selling more to the same customer | Selling to new customers | Increasing demand | Just buying it (inorganic) |

Let's walk through each one.

Selling More to the Same Customer

I believe the easiest way to generate more efficient sales for your business is to have your current customers buy more than one product from you. They are already a customer, and hopefully you have a good relationship with them. So why not increase the amount of money each customer spends with you? A study for the *Harvard Business Review* in 2014 cited that "acquiring a new customer is anywhere from five to twenty-five times more expensive than retaining an existing one."

This is also called increasing the share of wallet. This is classically defined as the amount of money that a customer spends with your brand versus a competing brand. By increasing your share of wallet with your customers, you not only generate more revenue from them, but you also crowd out dollars that would be going to the competition. And it's typically a heck of a lot easier (aka zero to low customer acquisition costs) to generate a sale from a current customer. There are several ways to approach this strategy, including bundling, upselling, and cross-selling.

Bundling is a great way to increase your customer lifetime value while providing your customers with a real or perceived benefit. It's a common strategy; everyone is familiar with the content programming done on cable and streaming TV. You can make a bundle out of everything. Each bundle has its own value to the consumer, the developer (if they own the content or product), or the aggregator. An example from earlier in this book is Expedia. Instead of just selling airline tickets, the company focused on bundling hotel and car content into a package. Increasing the share of wallet enabled Expedia to spend more money on customer acquisition (because the average order value increased) and ensured that a competitor didn't get the sale on another travel component.

Upselling is getting an existing customer to increase their spend with you by offering either more or an enhanced version of your product. If you are in technology, this strategy is very common for SaaS (software as a service) products. But it doesn't have to be B2B; you can use similar tactics in any market. For instance, your company may sell a small license to a very big company. Once you have your foot in the door, you can start to expand your sales volume inside this one customer. In many cases this is much more cost-effective than finding a new customer. In addition, you can try to upsell customers in many different ways. For instance, when I was in the gaming business, we would often offer customers discounted virtual coins with our social casino games. One of my favorite examples of all time is McDonald's. Who hasn't heard of the expression, "Supersize me!"

Cross-selling is selling complementary products to your existing customer base. You can decide to build or partner with new products or services that are effective for cross-selling. You can execute on this strategy in literally any type of business, whether it's consumer, SaaS, consulting, or really anything. These types of expansion strategies typically happen after you have established a relationship with your customers. When you do this effectively, you generate more value for the customers and can then get a higher lifetime value out of each one.

Of course, you can always offer new products to the same customer. This is not necessarily the same as bundling. The bundle explicitly includes multiple offerings priced at a lower total dollar value than the sum of the individual parts. The new product can be part of that bundle (e.g., inside an office productivity suite), or it can be sold separately to a customer with its own (non-bundled) price point.

A good example of cross-selling is Lexia Learning. Lexia was a company that Rosetta Stone bought in 2013 (we sold Rosetta Stone and Lexia as part of two transactions in late 2020 and early 2021). K to 12 student literacy is a huge problem, and Lexia is committed to solving it. In the US, for instance, two-thirds of third graders score below a proficient reading level (as defined by the federal government in their National Assessment of Educational Progress scores), and this trend continues through eighth grade. Lexia uses technology to empower educators to deliver proven results in literacy. The learning model is called blended learning, with students rotating between self-study with software, group reading, and one-on-one instruction. The software learns from the learner and is backed by thirty-five years of pedagogically sound literacy practice, with twenty evidence-based education research studies that show dramatic results in learner outcomes. Plainly put, their solution works.

Lexia had a high market penetration among younger students and a high penetration into about 10 percent of schools. The need for literacy software solutions didn't stop at younger students. Lexia saw a need for older students, which would also be a great fit to sell more products to districts that included grade schools, middle schools, and high schools. The team built a net-new product called PowerUp, which was targeted specifically at older students and could be sold by the same sales team. It enabled customers to use more of the Lexia literacy software, and it enabled more wallet share from younger to older students.

Nick Gaehde, president of Lexia Learning, examines how this strategy has worked for his business and, most importantly, how it has changed the lives of students:

Can you please explain your process and/or framework for making the decision to build PowerUp?

We looked at our customer base and who the purchasing decision-makers were. Often, we were talking to district-level curriculum directors who had responsibility for sourcing programs to support teachers and students from K to twelfth grade. We came to realize through many discussions with our customers that we were only meeting their needs when it came to elementary school students. We also realized that our unique capabilities in curriculum design could be applied to supporting the needs of middle and high school students. Although the needs were somewhat different in terms of building user interfaces that engaged older students and supporting teachers who may not have had training in the fundamentals of reading instruction, we also knew that our core methodology of blended learning and enabling the educator with real-time data could be applied to this student population. When considering product investments, we always prioritize new products that meet the needs of our current market or new markets that have a need for the products we have in our portfolio. These investments in product or channel typically have better returns than new products targeted at new markets.

How did PowerUp improve your business in terms of either net-new customers or account expansion?

One of the metrics we track carefully is the number of customers who have purchased more than one of our programs. These customers not only have higher average order sizes, but also higher retention rates and higher lifetime value. We have also found that we can have more conversations and purchases at the district level versus the school building level, because we are meeting a broader set of needs.

Did PowerUp help you defend your market position against the competition?

Our goal is to be the preferred partner for schools, school districts, and even state decision-makers when it comes to literacy instruction. This focus allows us to go deeper into meeting all literacy needs than our competitors who have chosen to build broad product portfolios across multiple subject domains. This focus and product depth supports our position as *the* literacy experts in the market.

NOTE THAT you don't have to build your own products to cross-sell. The extra products you sell don't have to be ones you built—you can cross-sell other products through revenue-share agreements with business partners. For instance, at Expedia, we had a healthy business of selling tours and attractions during the checkout process. Yes, we sold a lot of Vegas weddings.

Another example is from my business mentor Laurence Franklin, who was the CEO of premium luxury brands like TUMI and Coach. He had a strategy that he called "cheap and cheerful" initiatives. Selling brand-aligned products via partners can help you quickly get to market as well as increase your revenue.

Laurence and I spoke about how he has implemented those strategies:

Can you give me an example of how you have successfully deployed a partnership strategy?

The concept behind "cheap and cheerful" is that you enhance the impact of a program by adding a few simple, cost-effective touches. Imagine you're baking a cake with two layers. Most of the work goes into developing the recipe, creating the batter, and then baking those two layers—and of course, finishing with a great icing. Yet, by adding a third or even a fourth layer, you improve how enticing and tasty the cake is, with only a minor amount of additional effort.

Your company may be undertaking a marketing push in a particular region or segment of the market. Significant resources are likely required to ensure success. By adding a few "cheap and cheerful" elements, you can create even more impact. For example, layering on local PR placements will build awareness on top of any purchased media, especially in this age, where much of the media is seeking content. Partnering with one or two locally important organizations can also create a buzz whose value goes beyond the modest costs such initiatives require. With ESG [environmental, social, and governance] being an important trend, it is often simple to locate partners who genuinely and positively contribute to important issues, will appreciate the support you can provide them, and can help your brand create a presence way beyond the strict value of your financial investment.

At TUMI, we partnered with Matthew Modine and his "Bicycle for a Day" and "Waterkeeper" projects to enhance a nationwide product launch. His celebrity helped us obtain TV and other media coverage that normally would have been beyond our reach. This wasn't a paid product endorsement; we committed a modest percentage of revenues to the organizations he supported, and he gave us a little time.

In another arena, our product management team attended a trade show and noticed an item that was not on our radar nor part of our skill set, but that really fit with our brand because of its design and functionality. At the time, we were known for our travel and business bags and related accessories. The item was an electronics product. We developed a private label arrangement with the manufacturer, and with cosmetic touches (no engineering), we ensured the product looked sufficiently "TUMI" and brought it to market. It ended up being so successful, it led to a whole new category of products for us.

I'm also going to give you a couple of other examples of different types of alliances that had both commercial and strategic value. The objective was to leverage the power or the edginess of another brand to leapfrog our own brand into a different, more powerful dimension. Success would mean that as a result of the partnership, we would be perceived as a more relevant and dynamic brand and business. A double win would mean that we achieved strong commercial results to go along with enhanced brand impact.

At Coach, our B2B division developed a program with Lexus where Lexus would offer a "Coach Edition" version, and new owners of Lexus's most luxurious models would receive a set of Coach leather bags when they took possession of their car. At the time, Lexus was a relatively new brand. The public was well aware that Lexus was owned by Toyota, who had a tremendously strong position as a "value" player but no "luxury" brand credentials. Lexus had been provided significant marketing resources, but they recognized they couldn't buy consumer interest and acceptance—i.e., take market share—based on spend alone. Coach represented a partner that would enhance their credibility in the luxury market.

Our customers were their target audience. They were affluent, and equally important, they regarded us as authentic arbiters of quality, detailing, and good taste. In other words, they trusted us. Lexus understood the value we would bring at this crucial stage of their evolution. For Coach, this was a fabulous initiative because our partner not only paid for the product they bought, but they also featured us in a variety of high-quality media that drove millions of impressions. Alignment with the top Lexus vehicle, combined with the extensive investment they made in marketing and communications, brought us heightened awareness, provided our own marketing content a new "twist," and gave the brand a "wow" factor.

At TUMI, we initiated a partnership with Ducati, the Italian manufacturer of performance motorcycles. For a minor investment in product (valued at retail, not at cost) and a nominal license fee, we were able to build on the excitement and "stopping power" that a display of TUMI products with Ducati bikes engendered. In many international markets, where we were a fledgling brand, we were able to create pop-up displays or be featured in the windows of the most important local retailers, in addition to our own stores. The Ducati element meant we were no longer just a brand that designed good-looking, functional items—we were now "cool."

TUMI also created the amenity kits given out to first- and business-class flyers at Delta Air Lines. The commercial value of a kit that costs only a few dollars to a brand where many single items sell for five hundred or a thousand dollars is minimal. However, the marketing benefits of accessing tens of thousands of high-end customers are exceptional. We recognized that many of these customers would already be fans of the brand. To them, our offering reinforced our positioning as the premium brand for business travelers. To those who may have been aware of the brand but not yet customers, or just not aware, the arrangement delivered very effective lead-generation opportunities.

Each of these initiatives provided our marketing and PR groups with fabulous ammunition to create outreach and interesting content on a global basis. And we also had revenue from the limited-edition product lines that accompanied these ventures. The products themselves were modifications of our current offerings. We did not need to completely redesign or develop from scratch the associated products. Through detailing, trim, materials, and logo treatments, we created products that were definitely brand appropriate for us and for our partners.

I guess today what we did would be a form of affiliate marketing. But then it was just good strategy and tactics.

How do you decide which partners would be the right strategy fit for a cross-sell strategy?

Really good question. If your brand represents an attractive opportunity, there will frequently be companies or individuals looking to partner. I follow a five-tier process to help sift the good opportunities from the bad:

- You need to define if the potential relationship is a branding partnership or a supplier relationship. Are you borrowing the other entity's equity (co-branding), or are you utilizing their skills to bring products or services to market in an accelerated, cost-efficient fashion (make-versus-buy decision-making)? Both are fine, but you need to be clear on where the partnership value lies.

- You should be confident that the products and services the partner (business, brand, organization, person) offers represent a value set (actual and perceived) that matches your own brand equities.

- Do you see sufficient cultural similarities between your organization and that of the potential partner to enable mutual goodwill, responsiveness, and support for the initiative?

- Will this arrangement create significant value? How? What does success look like?

- Are you as important to the partner as they are to you?

There should be clear answers to all these questions, with enough specificity to both motivate and engage each side's teams, and to help ensure the program's success.

What are some things to avoid when building out your partnership strategy?

An equally important question. What is key when engaging with partners is support and alignment within your business. Unless all key participants are committed to the venture's success, things can fall apart really easily.

Being cognizant of team bandwidth and resource availability is also important. This applies to all projects, but especially to those where you're dependent on outsiders.

Unless the building blocks for success are in place in both organizations, the project will have a troubled path, and outcomes will be suboptimal. As with most opportunities, the ideas are the easy part—it's the execution that makes (or breaks) an initiative.

Partnerships are an obvious strategy that's often overlooked. You can also license content, other products, etc. You can bundle these products together, include them in your shopping cart, and even execute on mutual bundling strategies. You can build deeper business development relationships that are longer lasting when you start to share economic benefit between two or more parties.

Selling to New Customers

There are countless books that review the best way to test and build new products. That is outside the scope of this book. You can create a new product in the same market for a different customer or take the same product with the same customer and sell it in a new market. There are several ways in which you can think about selling to new customers. They include geography, segment, and channel.

Geography: Let's start with one of the most capital-intensive ways to think about selling: geographic expansion. If you have outgrown an existing market or simply see an advantage in another market, then take the proverbial show on the road and expand internationally.

You can "lift" your business from one market and put it in another market. Now, before you roll your eyes on how it's harder than it looks, the answer is, of course, "it depends." Some horizontal solutions can be localized effectively in different markets. This has been done successfully in travel and gaming, as with game and movie franchises like *Fortnite* and *Candy Crush*. Technology-oriented players like Amazon and Uber have more or less the same look and feel, with some localized inventory and offers. Software distribution has made much of this a heck of a lot easier as well. Many brands also structure partnerships in the form of joint ventures, where you work with local partners that can provide the local expertise, connections, and capital to make your product a success. Look at Yum! Brands, who own fast-food brands like KFC, Pizza Hut, and Taco Bell. They created a successful entity in China that is run as a completely unique and separate publicly traded business.

Segment: You can decide to focus on different segments of a B2B market (aka firmographics) or a different customer (demographics or psychographics). Instead of going after just small business, you can decide to build solutions for larger customers. For instance, at Rosetta Stone, we adapted our adult learning product into an enterprise product.

On the really, really net-new side, you want to make sure that your proposition is solving a real customer problem. You don't want to waste your time and capital on a product that doesn't. There are ways in which you can test your ideas even before you build a new product; we walked through these in Part Two: Timing earlier in the book.

It can be difficult to build a net-new product for a net-new audience. Hopefully you have the right team in place that is good at building net-new products. Your options for this require a lot of thought and attention on where you spend your time. If you can architect it, it's much better to bootstrap some advantage to a net-new customer. That advantage can be a brand, some product expertise—something to leverage is ideal.

Channel: There are many different approaches to channel. You can decide to expand your sales directly or indirectly. Here is a quick summary of some ways to think about channel expansion:

- **Direct:** This involves direct sales from a website, a direct sales force, etc.

- **Indirect:** Use a reseller. This is a broad moniker; basically, it's a term for a seller or retail organization that sells the product on your behalf. Think about a third-party e-commerce (website), an app store, an off-line store (e.g., grocery store, department store, etc.), or a value-added reseller (a company that integrates your solution with another set of products and services).

Increasing Demand

Drive more customers to your product! Be wary of how effective your marketing is; you do not want to spend more on your customer acquisition than the lifetime value of your customer. If you are an online business, you have a ton of paid and organic (free) ways to do this. There are so many ways to grow your traffic that we will not have the proper space to explain them all here. You have several options, including:

- **Paid:** Options range from Google AdWords, Facebook ads, video advertising on streaming TV, etc.

- **Organic:** This includes free traffic from search engines via search engine optimization (SEO), word of mouth, and public relations.

- **Product-led:** This involves building viral features into your product or service so that customers are referred to your product and/or service.

There's a lot to cover here, but be mindful of the mix of your traffic. Being too reliant on paid marketing over time can be costly. It could also be a sign that your product over-indexes on new customers, which could tell you that it isn't sticky.

Understanding the core economic metrics from your lifetime value per customer and your customer acquisition costs is critical. Often you can even decide not to do something based on the customer acquisition cost—meaning that it's simply too expensive to acquire a customer, especially if you look into your crystal ball and divine that the customer acquisition costs are only going to get more expensive over time.

Just Buying It

Building a business from scratch is very hard. Sometimes buying a business is better. Depending on your capital situation, if you need to enter a market quickly and/or need to add a business to your arsenal to help satisfy more of the market wants and needs, buying a business could be just the right move.

To go back to Expedia as an example, as an intermediary in the travel business, having some influence related to the size of the pie that you control becomes really important. Size does matter. The bigger you are, the more difficult it is to turn you off. Expedia (formerly owned by Internet conglomerate IAC) purchased a slew of companies to give the business more advantage, both from a demand as well as a supply perspective. For instance, over a short time frame the company purchased Hotels.com, Hotwire, Classic Vacations, Egencia, and many more. That gave the business some leverage with the sources of traffic—in particular, it made us one of the biggest adversaries of Google (and Google has always been a threat for intermediaries, by displacing them and getting consumers to book directly in the search engine). The other advantage was supply. Having more business inventory with a hotel, car, or air provider enables better pricing and more influence over inventory.

KEY TAKEAWAYS FROM THIS CHAPTER

There are four operating dials that can really help you focus your plan. They are not mutually exclusive.

Here are some key highlights from this chapter:

- Sell more to the same customer (by cross-selling and upselling). The best way to both expand your sales and crowd out the competition is to sell more products and services to the same customer. The three approaches are to bundle, upsell, and cross-sell. You do not have to rely solely on building a new product, either. Third-party partnerships are a completely viable way to generate net incremental sales without having to build your own product for cross-selling.

- Sell to new customers—this is always a viable approach. Three options to look at are geography, segment, and channel. Geographic expansion is the most difficult approach because it usually requires extensive local market support as well as a lot of capital.

- Increase demand—if your business is working, then put some more gas on it! Just be mindful of your customer acquisition costs, and have a firm handle on your customer lifetime value.

- Just buy it (inorganic)—if you have a business that can be bolstered by another business (and you can finance it), buying another business makes a ton of sense. It can also help you strategically block the competition and lock in customers.

7

IMPROVING YOUR CUSTOMER VALUE PROPOSITION

THIS SECTION IS a bit more prescriptive due to my personal experience as a product manager. It's critical that your team focuses on the product in a way that is aligned with your strategy. I like to build what I call a "north star" framework that aligns what you're going to build to the customer's wants and needs. If you do this correctly, everyone is aligned from every echelon in the company. One way to do this is to create a product management framework to help organize your decisions.

There are many frameworks to use, and we will walk through several of them below. The bigger the company, the more detailed and thoughtful you have to be with your planning—there's just more complexity and more teams pulling on a finite set of resources. Smaller companies are a lot easier—it's so obvious what to do next that you don't even need to do meetings and planning. You just need to make your choice, hopefully based on the stage and size of your organization.

First, Start with Your North Star

I have heavily borrowed my personal planning style from Atlassian, the company that makes development tools like Jira and Confluence. For my planning, I like to start with a vision (or "north star") that aligns the entire company with the business's true purpose. I then like to build out key themes that support that vision. A theme can be used as a criterion, meaning that it can help you focus on the top three or four areas you are going to work on, to create customer delight and consequently business advantage.

The framework that Atlassian uses for this—and which I have used in the companies I have run—is the VTFM framework. VTFM stands for:

- **Vision:** This refers to the big picture and the opportunity the product is aiming for. Great vision statements are clear about the market as well as the customer they are trying to serve.

- **Themes:** As mentioned above, these are the core three to four areas that drive customer delight and adoption.

- **Focus areas:** These are the specific ideas and features that deliver on the themes and are generally delivered (in the best organizations) from customers' unmet needs.

- **Measures:** These are the metrics that will help to guide your teams as they create guideposts for success with your feature rollout and adoption.

I love this framework because once you agree on the themes, everything else in terms of business planning and product development becomes a natural extension to them. It also aligns your product teams with the goal in the product. In the software world, if your developers are very closely aligned to the goals, they are going to be really focused on obtaining those key outcomes. At the end of the day, the goal is to deliver exceptional customer value. So the idea is to build products that do this—"epic" products that get customers driving organic word-of-mouth traction for your product.

Once you have this framework laid out, you can start to plan out your year. I like to chunk out my planning in all things on a quarterly basis. Use the themes to guide what you work on and a framework (per the above) to help you plan out what you are going to ship. I like to use a weighted model that looks at the total capacity for the quarter. I split the overall effort against each theme. Then the product team can make their initial recommendations on the areas to focus on for the upcoming quarter.

Once we have agreed on the north star and themes, I like to keep the planning process very focused on results, to let teams stay focused on making their own decisions to deliver exceptional customer value. An additional tip to ensure that you provide maximum value and maximum empowerment is to set up a rhythm of regular check-ins—or, if you will, implement a "trust but verify" approach. You want to have empowered teams. I always believe that if you are building customer-centric products, it's good to build in a cadence for review to ensure that everything is aligned. This can take many forms, but here is how I have approached it:

Create a Customer Value Road Map

There are several prioritization frameworks you could use when building out your product road map. Regardless of which one you choose, the main focus is to ensure that you are building products that a) customers will pay for and b) customers will continue to use (and buy). This may sound obvious, but too often I see product plans that are not customer-centric. I am often reminded of the prescient words of Warren Buffett's partner, Charlie Munger: "One of our directors said, very simply, 'We should make a list of everything that irritates the customer, and then we should eliminate those defects one by one.' That is the way to compete in a service business."

Here is a quick overview of a couple of the customer-centric prioritization frameworks that are worth looking into. They include:

- **Value versus complexity:** This is one of my favorite frameworks because it's so simple. It gives product teams a disciplined, simple, and objective way to prioritize features. The scoring mechanism is simple, and you can easily plot the output of your decisions. It works particularly well when you have a long list of features and functionality.

- **Benefit versus cost (weighted scoring):** This is another good framework. It's a bit more complicated than value versus complexity. You pick benefit and cost variables to weight, which allows you to prioritize your criteria. Typically, you have a list of different criteria that you can build as a theme, such as "increase engagement," "speed and performance," etc. This model is great when you have a larger organization with more product complexity and more buy-in needs.

One of the different approaches to weighting (and there are many) is weighting all your requests by theme but also by feasibility, desirability, and viability. This idea was cooked up by the design powerhouse IDEO about twenty years ago. It's an interesting approach because you can get a Goldilocks of building functionality that is just right. A higher score is typically better. A quick way to think about it is via "FDV":

- **Feasible:** Is it a solution that your team can currently pull off? For instance, if you are really good at building mobile apps that are engaging, then building some new feature that leverages that team's strength is highly feasible. The alternative is, let's say, you don't have a plan for sustaining life on Mars, yet you are sending humans to Mars—most likely not a very feasible solution.

- **Desirable:** Is it functionality that really addresses a customer pain point? Desirability solves the pain point and delights the customer.

- **Viable:** Does the functionality support your long-term business model? You could end up making some short-term decisions that positively impact short-term financial results, but that could also build negative consequences for customers longer term.

A Product Plan Example

Let's take a real-world example. From the VTFM, let's say that I built out three key themes for my business. Engagement is one of these themes. The higher the engagement is, the better the natural rate of renewal should be, which is vital for a subscription product.

A Product Plan Example

PROJECT			FDV SCORE—1 IS BAD, 5 IS GOOD			
Product Theme	Customer Pain/Gain	Hypotheses/ Solutions	Feasible	Desirable	Viable	Total
Simplify Account Creation	**Pain:** Customers unwilling to create accounts. • 40–45% of our users' app downloads do not create an account. Some are not willing to provide an email address, or it is not convenient to type it in. • 82–87% of users who are exposed to a free trial on the website do not create an account. **Gain:** Evidence that a material portion of web users prefer using social accounts. • Social sign-in has been reported to increase sign-in conversion up to 40%.	Social sign-in support (Facebook, Google, possibly Apple)	3	3	4	10

You can see that in order to organize everything, I have the product theme (from the VTFM). Most importantly, I have explicitly stated the customer pain/gain. Remember, we are building a customer-centric product solution. You then have a sense of the solution and scoring. There are many approaches to what I call "definition of ready." This means that someone has done the work to validate that what you are building actually nails a customer benefit. There are many ways to do this, including focus groups, research, live testing of "fake" screens, etc. The point is that you know enough about whether your hypothesis about the product works before you actually build it. It's not your job to be a micro-manager, but it is your job to ensure that your team is not building to ideas that are not addressing customer wants and needs.

Heck, I have done every version of this exercise. Like I said earlier, you can be as simple or as exhaustive as you like. Here is another example of a very simple prioritization process. I used this template at one of my previous startups.

Super Simple Product Planning

	BENEFIT Rank 1–5 (1 = Lowest, 5 = Highest)			SCORE	
Initiative	Differentiation	Growth	Engagement	Implementation Cost Rank 1–5 (1 = Highest, 5 = Lowest)	Total Score
Feature	4	2	3		
Feature	4	4	5		
Feature	1	2	3		
Feature	1	1	3		
Feature	1	5	2		

Sometimes simpler is better. I have done this using Google Sheets, so the entire company can see our prioritization. I have every feature for a product listed, then give each one a simple ranking score of 1 to 5 for various benefits. Add up your benefits times your cost and voilà, the highest score wins.

Be open about how you prioritize feedback. You should open up to your team(s) about your thinking about priorities and product. Invite them into the decision-making process. You want to have as many diverse voices review your plan as possible—that ensures less groupthink and enables you to wring out every perspective. I have found that customer service, sales, account management—really, anyone who is talking to customers on a regular basis—have the best understanding of the wants and needs of your customers.

Measure Twice, Cut Once: Get Buy-Off

Your product team should always be articulating the next set of features and services they plan to work on. I like to do this forty-five days before the end of the quarter. This gets everyone comfortably thinking ahead and on the same page.

I like to get a review and approval on the set of card-level features. What I mean by "card level" is significant features, not minor items like bug fixes. The objective is to get approval on larger initiatives by theme to ensure that everyone is aligned. I confess I am a tad anal-retentive on measuring the approach to building customer value. To each their own. Ignore this advice if the style doesn't fit with your culture.

This might be a lot of detail, but being vigilant on how the product team delivers value versus the business strategy is so important. Here is how I structure the process:

- **Review "big" features.** Any major feature that is "significant" (over some predetermined point total) needs to be reviewed for its market demand and likely acceptance by customers. Demand data on functionality that has not been fully built (whether it's in the product or via primary research). Examples are "product pull testing" (click/tap demand for features, sample customer acquisition tests, etc.). You are creating tests to see if customers show interest in early versions of product concepts. Also look for primary research, focus groups, etc. (these are not mutually exclusive). Customer, competitive, and stakeholder feedback should be included as part of this meeting. I assume that there's always a continuous feedback loop between the customer and the people building the product.

- **Determine your principles.** I like to have these stated somewhere in the road map. They must conform to the strategy. I always take a special look toward the feature requests that have the product team create customized features or have the customer take a product in a bespoke direction. For example, a common use case is that corporate customers really need some unique customization, and the deal could be huge in terms of potential annual recurring revenue. Do you take the money now (because you need it) and risk taking your previous engineering resources off in a direction that isn't strategically aligned with your long-term strategy? Every operator has had to answer this type of question across any vertical. It's best to have a strong perspective—otherwise you will be guided by every tactical customer request, which will ensure that you don't invest in the right initiatives for your business in the long term.

- **Let the doer present.** The product manager and the designer should be available to make their case. The people that do the work and who are closest to the customer should be the ones presenting *their* own work.

KEY TAKEAWAYS FROM THIS CHAPTER

Being thoughtful about a customer-centric value proposition combines inspiration with tons of planning. With the proper application, you will be able to naturally build epic products and services to unlock new or existing value in your business.
Here are some key highlights from this chapter:

- You have now built a compelling north star. You have integrated your product vision with the business vision. You have identified three or four key themes for your service that are customer-benefit aligned. You have thought about the measures (key outcomes) you will hold yourself and your teams accountable to in order to show progress toward delighting your customers. I prefer the VTFM approach, but feel free to dream up your own.

- You have developed a process. You have built out some form of customer-centric prioritization process, one that is appropriate for ingesting feedback from customers, internal stakeholders, and your own inspired vision. There is a range of options for how to do this, from simple to complex. Pick the one that is right for the size of your organization and the complexity of your product.

- You should regularly review your plan. Things change. You are getting feedback on a quarterly basis on priorities that support the key themes in your business. You are enabling the team to present their own ideas and are making sure that the plan makes sense and is aligned with your business goals.

8

COMMUNICATING YOUR PLAN

"IF A TREE FALLS in a forest and no one is around to hear it, does it make a sound?" is a philosophical thought experiment that raises questions about observation and perception. Without getting too metaphysical, my response is a categorical, "Hell no!"

This section discusses concepts like "operating dials" and other planning elements, which can tend to sound very consulting-like. Trust me, I am not a consultant. All of these frameworks are super important, and eventually you will need to simplify them so that everyone understands them.

This chapter sort of slipped into the book by accident, because communication isn't technically a factor in determining whether you can unlock value in your company. However, establishing a strong culture and focusing on your people is absolutely a key component to executing on your plan. Plans need to be clear, but they also need to be scaled broadly and openly. Everyone in the organization should be able to understand the vision, mission, and cultural values of a business with their eyes closed.

Vision, Mission, and Big Hairy Audacious Goals

Your team wants to be led. Great businesses construct a compelling vision of the future that invites employees, investors, and customers to join the adventure with them.

Of course, we can't go much further on this subject without reciting the guru on the subject, Jim Collins. In his exceptional book *Built to Last*, Collins writes about how a vision is actually a formula made up of two parts: a core ideology plus an envisioned future. The envisioned future is called a Big Hairy Audacious Goal or BHAG. The BHAG is a clear, descriptive goal that will take a long time to achieve—say, ten to thirty years.

Collins details the power of having a clear and compelling goal. I have always liked the research-based sensibility to his writing. What has always stood out to me is that he talks about how much better companies with compelling BHAGS perform than what he calls "comparison" companies. The BHAG is like a company's "moon mission." When written well, it hits you in the gut. It's so clear and compelling that people "get it" right away; it takes little to no explanation.

First let's focus on the vision statement, which is an expression of what tomorrow should look like and what your organization wants to ultimately become. Again, Collins breaks it down into a core ideology plus an envisioned future. The core ideology is made up of "core values" and a "core purpose." Values are guiding principles; they express how you act as a company.

Think about yourself—what drives you, and what are your core intrinsic motivators? Me, I am about integrity, passion, freedom, and fun. I look for companies that share those values aligned with a compelling vision of the future (or purpose). That is why cultural values are important. They attract like-minded fellow adventurers to your vision and set the parameters on how you behave. Those values become the basis for a compelling culture. The culture is how the company lives through its values in practice.

The second component of a vision statement is the core purpose. This is, as Collins puts it, a company's "most fundamental reason for being." Here are some famous examples of BHAGs:

- **IKEA:** "Our vision is to create a better everyday life for the many people."

- **Apple:** "To make the best products on earth, and to leave the world better than we found it."

- **Nike:** "Bring inspiration and innovation to every athlete* in the world. (*If you have a body, you are an athlete.)"

- **Google:** "To provide access to the world's information in one click."

- **Rosetta Stone:** "Every person can learn to read, write, and speak with confidence."

Now, let's chat about BHAGs (the envisioned future). You want the BHAG and the vision to be closely related. Think of BHAGs as an extension of the vision statement. I think companies spend too much time focusing on the architecture of their messaging and not enough on the actual messaging. So for me, the BHAG and the core vision are closely aligned.

Otherwise, you have to draft two different sorts of compelling long-term destinations for your company.

I like to have a simple call to action that is a farsighted goal that supports the company's vision. I like to tie specific methods or initiatives that align the company's focus with supporting that goal. To me, the shorter the better. Human beings already have too much on their minds. Don't ask us to remember some corporate jargoning statement. Make it short and impactful.

There are all sorts of BHAGs. Some are competitive, and some are financial. I like to make my BHAG personal— something that really gets the troops excited to compete or is targeted at a number that is a big stretch.

Earlier in the book, I mentioned that the former CEO of Expedia's vision was to be "the largest seller of travel online." Once we had accomplished that, we changed it to being the "largest seller of travel in the world." The CEO used Travelocity, number one in online travel at the time, as a focal point for our efforts, and then switched to American Express, the largest seller of travel off-line and online at the time. Some other famous BHAGs:

- "Crush Adidas." (Nike in the 1960s)

- "We will destroy Yamaha." (Honda in the 1970s)

- "Become a $125 billion company by year 2000." (Walmart in 1990)

- And my favorite: "A computer on every desk and in every home." (Bill Gates, Microsoft, 1975)

You want your BHAG to become a rallying cry that is right for your organization. It has to fit culturally. For instance, who could forget Gerard Butler in the role of King Leonidas in the 2007 movie *300*? Imagine having a crazy, aggressive rallying cry akin to his famous scream, "This is Sparta!"—but used within a children's education company. *No bueno.*

Lastly, let's move to the mission statement. If a vision statement is the heart of a company, the mission statement is the head. Many people mix up vision statements and mission statements or think they're somehow the same thing, but they are very different. A lot of companies like to have both a vision and a mission statement (and a BHAG). I get why. The vision is your unique perspective on your company's role in the world. A mission statement is more practical—it focuses on today and what an organization plans to do to achieve its strategic goals. Both are vital in directing resources as well as inspiring your team.

Here's the difference between a vision and a mission statement, using Nike as an example:

- **Nike's vision:** "Bring inspiration and innovation to every athlete in the world."

- **Nike's mission:** "To do everything possible to expand human potential. We do that by creating groundbreaking sport innovations, by making our products more sustainably, by building a creative and diverse global team, and by making a positive impact in communities where we live and work."

Many companies have fantastically hard-to-remember goals. When I worked in HR measuring employee engagement, I was always surprised at the number of world-class companies, big and small, that did *not* have a clear and compelling rallying cry.

Putting a Framework around Your Vision

Having a compelling vision transcends the day-to-day grind and gives real meaning to everyone's work. But don't stop there! Continue to atomize your plan into years, quarters, months, and weeks. Make it a part of the drumbeat of everything you do. That way, everyone's goals can be directly tied into your plan. This "operating system" then reinforces itself, and the performance compounds over time.

One of the operating frameworks I like to use is something that I basically stole from Salesforce. It's their V2MOM framework, which stands for Vision, Values, Methods, Obstacles, and Measures. I adopted it since it reinforces the long-term vision, and it scales goal setting. I added a "G" for Goals, to create a "V2GMOM" framework.

I have always thought of Salesforce as a personal mentor and have found Marc Benioff to be a fascinatingly iconoclastic leader. Salesforce's framework is very simple to articulate, and it drives everyone in the same direction. I have my teams set quarterly OKR-style goals (Objectives and Key Results) against the framework.

You can easily highlight key activities under each method with specific measures. The V2GMOM is an easy framework for your annual plan. This framework can be used over multiple years and can support your vision and your BHAG. I even have my one-on-ones (1:1s) in the V2GMOM framework, so that we are always holding ourselves accountable to the plan.

So let's break down how to use the framework:

Vision: This represents what you want to achieve. We have already spent a lot of time on this in the section above. This is the place to copy and paste your vision right into the document. Amazon wouldn't be the place it is today if it thought about its vision as being the largest bookseller in the world—its actual vision is "to build a place where people can come to find and discover anything they might want to buy online."

Values: Values are the principles or beliefs that are most important to your organization as you pursue your vision. They guide how your organization behaves, hires, makes decisions, etc. The values are your code, and your culture is a manifestation of them. You can see from the example above that these values are blasé and bland. They could pretty much be used for any company. For instance, how many times have you seen "integrity" as a company value? Well, who doesn't want to have integrity in their organization?

I personally like to have bespoke values that lean a little toward the colloquial. I love how the CEO of Twilio, Jeff Lawson, thinks about designing their cultural values. He talks about writing values using nouns versus adjectives. They have ten cultural values, and they are very unique (as all great cultural values should be) to Twilio. For example, one of their cultural values is "draw the owl." This has a fun backstory and is designed to convey that there's no instruction book, nor will anyone at the company tell you how to do your work. They want to hire team members who are empowered.

Goals and methods: These are the initiatives that represent how you will achieve your vision. If you look through Salesforce's methods, they obviously did the 1.0 version. These were created at the dawn of the company.

I personally like to bucket my methods under goals. I am also a fan of creating a balanced scorecard that buckets my methods under four categories: employees/team, product, financial, and customer. That way, everyone in the organization can think about impacting each goal in some form. For instance, not everyone in a company influences a financial goal, but certainly everyone can better support a customer or become a better manager.

I like to have no more than three to four goals and two to three methods per goal. Think of methods as the objectives for achieving a particular goal. But you do not have to use goals with the V2MOM framework. I do it to have everyone on the team think about the four vectors (employees, product, financial, and customer). It's your choice. In essence, the methods are the key ways of achieving your measure. You can use the "measure," which we will talk about below, as the goal too.

Obstacles: I always find that having radical candor and transparency is the key to establishing engagement at your company, as this leads to trust. To me, obstacles are the ultimate expression of candor. These are the items that will block your progress to achieving your goals and methods. For instance, if you are trying to hire thirty developers before the end of the quarter but you are not able to pay a competitive rate, that obstacle should be identified so that it can be addressed.

Measures: These are the specific yardsticks that articulate how you gauge your success. For goal setting (using SMART goals or OKRs), think of a measure as your goal. An example is: "Achieve a market share of 50 percent in the US consumer language-learning market by the end of the year."

Communicate Constantly

Being able to set and articulate a long-term vision and goal enables you and your team to do the seemingly impossible. I personally like mine to be so simple that anyone can remember it. I used to compare my articulated plays to the

Subway jingle for the five-dollar footlong sandwich commercial because it's so easy to remember. You need to constantly communicate your vision and plan. Everyone is busy, and your entire organization needs to be reminded of your true goal on a continual basis. If you are a leader, communicating should be a large component of how you spend your time.

We all have better communication tools today than many years ago. Building a healthy habit of creating a system of communication also reinforces to your entire company the progress of your business and enables you to be more flexible without being a control freak. Here are some ideas that I personally follow in the organizations I run.

Business Processes

Annual plan and quarterly review: I do an annual plan. It takes the form of the V2GMOM. I usually have an offsite that includes my core executive team to draft the V2GMOM. We review the plan on a quarterly basis with a wider group of executives, where we adjust initiatives and methods based on what's working or not.

Monthly reviews: I typically have each larger team or unit present their progress on a monthly basis. The format is simple and follows their committed quarterly plan. Materials are sent twenty-four hours in advance.

Board meetings: All of these materials are building toward the eventual quarterly meeting with your board and/or investors. Since I am always reviewing the business, the business operators do not have to generate a lot of new material—the board meetings are being written every week.

Product planning: I am used to two-week product engineering sprints (where work is chunked out on a recurring set of small tasks). We empower teams but generally help to allocate points by theme every quarter. I typically tie our annual product planning to our strategic planning so that everyone is aligned. I do like to have a kickoff on major products and a "definition of done" meeting before something larger goes live. I am in those reviews.

Internal financing through stage gates: There are always tests with features, pricing, etc. The key is to not have executives involved with a lot of decisions. But you should build out your processes so you can get a sense of what is going on. I like to encourage marketing teams to publish their tests. Marketing should always be testing and thinking about testing, just like a product team thinks about testing new ideas. Each test has a null hypothesis, and the team is empowered to show their progress.

Stage gates are important to help you frame an investment. Too many times you see companies build products that do not materialize as successes in the real world. They can spend millions of dollars on something that doesn't work. I like to agree with the internal teams on what success looks like across several stages. Each element along the way is reviewed so that the next stage gets its funding. Each team usually shows the data when they are ready to show it. I like to think of this as a venture model where teams define what success looks like so that they can raise more funding for their projects. This can be done for anything—not just for product. For example, at Rosetta Stone, we had a view that we should increase our TV advertising spend. The team built out a detailed plan and performance thresholds so that we could track the progress on a weekly basis based on the return of that cohorted spend.

Reinforce, Reinforce, Reinforce

It takes consistent messages on a continual and persistent basis for those discrete themes to stick in your teams' brains. I try to reinforce the company vision and goals all the time in both informal and formal ways. Here are some examples of what I do:

Town halls: Every month or so, we do a town hall meeting. The key to town halls is to celebrate your team first. I always like to announce promotions, job anniversaries, and recognition for exceptional work. I start out every meeting with our vision and then jump right into the team. I ask for questions in advance so that employees can ask questions anonymously and have them answered during the meeting. I also share the answers on an internal HR portal. We typically cover business updates, customer wins, and maybe a special presentation or two from the product, marketing, or HR teams.

Drumbeat communication: Slack, Confluence, email, etc. I view these modes of operation as reinforcement to the key plays in our V2GMOM. I also like to reinforce in these channels anything related to our culture, including diversity, equity, and inclusion. The tone of your leadership sets the tone for your company and reinforces your cultural values. So please remember to be authentic. Employees can smell an insincere communication or gesture from a digital mile away.

Office hours: I do periodic virtual office hours. I did this before COVID-19 hit. The world is only going to go more remote in the future, and your key talent is often not going to be in your office or time zone. But human beings still crave human connection. I encourage a more formal set of interactions where ideas can be shared and questions asked. This requires leaders to be more transparent. Also, you definitely need to change your style to be more forthcoming in a remote-first world.

One-on-ones (1:1s): You need to do these every week with your direct reports. And if you can allocate the time, have the occasional meeting with your directs' directs (the people that report to your directs). A best practice that I have adopted over time is that I do open one-on-ones. My team aligns our updates to our V2GMOM in one doc. This saves time on staff updates and tactical detail that I or a cross-functional team may not need to carefully review, and it helps reduce long and boring staff meetings. Anyone can comment on each other's work. We read about issues and discuss them. There are no needless activity updates that eat up time and don't help a broad group. Keep one-on-ones focused on supporting your team, removing obstacles, and getting time and energy on track.

Scorecards: These should be very simple, no more than one or two numbers. For investors and boards, I like to reinforce my goals in a simple format so that they understand how we are trending in a balanced manner. I touched on this approach above by covering employees, product, financial, and customer metrics. For my inside team, I like to make it super simple and catchy. For example, I might tie a bookings number for the year to key strategic concepts. The litmus test is that it should be easy enough for anyone to remember at a moment's notice.

Scale Your Principles, Empower Your People

I work my teams very hard, and I openly talk about it. I am a big fan of creating management onboarding and continual reinforcement, especially for managers, on both how to do their job and on creating a blueprint to define their overall success. I like to create a management philosophy that is available everywhere and reinforced constantly. Empowerment becomes infectious—that is the basis for much of my work with leadership teams.

Employee Satisfaction: Keeping You and Leadership in Check

I view my team as the most important piece of my business. As I have said before, if you have a high-functioning, talented team, they will take care of your customers and generate long-term value for your company in turn. You need to be listening to your teams as much as you listen to your customers. Here are some easy ways to keep yourself aligned with your teams:

Employee satisfaction polling: Poll your employees on a regular cadence. Keep the poll down to two questions with an area for open feedback. The two questions I would recommend are: "Please rate your level of satisfaction at work" and "On a scale of 0 to 10, how likely are you to recommend <our company> to a friend or colleague?"

I find that quarterly polling works best, since you want to make sure that you can dedicate time to review the results and put an action plan on areas of focus. Keep the score transparent—this means available to everyone. Prioritize the feedback, and openly discuss areas you want to focus on and others that you simply cannot address. Being honest with your "no's" is better than saying "we will consider your feedback" when it isn't true.

Recognition: Recognition is the least used but most powerful cheap incentive I have ever seen. Building a system of feedback and a culture of "thank you" does a tremendous job of reinforcing intrinsically good performance, and it also shows other employees the behaviors that are needed to become recognized. You can build paid incentives and contests, or simply have a system where you regularly recognize rock star behavior without an award. Make it a habit to celebrate the managers and the team members in your regular town halls and communications. All of this reinforces good habits and publicly shows what it takes to be successful. This is how you reinforce cultural values.

KEY TAKEAWAYS FROM THIS CHAPTER

It isn't good enough to have a plan that is well crafted—the plan must become a living component of the daily, weekly, monthly, quarterly, and annual activity of your business.

To ensure that you have alignment, consider the following key highlights from this chapter:

- Develop a compelling vision, mission, and BHAG (Big Hairy Audacious Goal). Companies with aspirational long-term visions perform better. You can keep and attract talent more easily, and your strategic plans have a better shot of coming to fruition.

- Have a plan framework. Build out a simple framework for one and three years in the future. Align the plan with quarterly goal setting and reviewing the specific methods on a regular basis, in case you need to do more or less of those particular efforts.

- Communicate your plan and its progress regularly. Build a cadence of formal and informal habits and ceremonies that communicate your vision, goals, and strategies. Curate it to your unique culture.

- Regularly poll your internal stakeholders on their satisfaction. Publish your findings and the discussion of your action plan on how you will remediate your most important priorities. Be honest about what you are *not* planning to focus on. Employees will want to know the "why" of your decision-making. You can't satisfy everyone, but you can establish trust, which drives engagement and loyalty.

- Recognize your team. Recognition can be as simple as nonfinancial awards. But the key is to make it public. That encourages more of the behavior you are recognizing from the team member *and* from the team members not being recognized.

HOW WOULD YOU SCORE THIS SECTION?

It's time to score your second piece of the Insight Score on "Planning." If you are in the right place at the right time and have an offering that is working in the marketplace, that's more than half the battle—but you need a strategic plan. Out of all the questions to score, building a better plan is the most controllable. You can always refine your plan, change it, and get help with it.

INSIGHT QUESTION #4
Do you have an executable plan?

How to score this question:

- Not yet—still working. (1 pt.)
- Got a plan, no resources. (2 pts.)
- We are ready to *go*! (3 pts.)

On to the next question!

FIVE

MOMENTUM AND YOUR KEY INSIGHT

How confident are you that you
can attract the talent and
resources needed to pull this off?

9

USING YOUR TEAM TO CREATE/ BUILD MOMENTUM

Talent Drives Momentum

Momentum really moves the needle for the Insight Score. It has a multiplier effect in the T3PM calculation (TAM + Timing + Track Record + Plan × Momentum). You can have the best-laid plans, but if you do not have the capital and the team to execute on them, then you can kiss your dreams goodbye. In an early-stage company, most investors are laser-beam focused on the team. There's no data, there's no revenue, and the product might not even exist yet. It's all about the team, and the investor is trying to decide if the entrepreneur has the grit and talent to start to make their grand vision into a reality. As your business grows, you're going to need different types of people. For example, the brilliant founder who's technical may not be the right skilled CEO over the long term.

Eventually, I'd like to see more data-driven human resources practices in all companies. Since everything is being measured through software, I am not sure why we don't have more manager automation tools, such as tools to help us determine what to do at certain times of stage growth, scaling management best practices, etc. I would recommend reading and listening to Josh Bersin, a global human resources research analyst. He does a great job articulating what the future of work looks like, and he has a technology bent to his perspectives.

This book is not meant to be an authority on human resources. However, you need to have a perspective and a set of frameworks so you can evaluate your team in the context of being positioned as a market leader. This section is going to cover the following ideas:

- Team-centric metrics.
- Organizational future state.
- Reviewing talent depth—is it the right team?
- Evaluating diversity—of talent, products, and personality.

I believe that your team is the most important asset in your business. If you're large enough to hire a human resources professional, you should be treating that person as one of your most important right-hand leaders. Over time, as you and your leaders deal with constant growth, you will need to focus more on your team. Making sure that you have a smart, talented, and culturally aligned group is very important for the long haul.

Measures to Track Your Talent

You and your management team should be tracking some pretty common team metrics. If your company is too small and you are laughing as you read this, trust me, that is a good problem to have—and you'll be big enough someday that you will say to yourself, "I wish I had tracked these metrics more closely."

I like to look at my team metrics on par with my financial metrics. I'm always a fan of looking at metrics on a continuous basis as a macro indicator, since your team really drives the results, and the hunger for great talent is getting more competitive. You do not have the luxury of resting on your proverbial laurels with a feedback mechanism that is only annual. Employee data must be real-time, continuous, and built into the culture of your company.

Some of these indicators are easy to measure (we will walk through a sample). Others are more subtle and could be more specific to the type of business you're building. For instance, if you're building a services company, you don't care about how many engineers you need to hire. By the way, if you do a broad search on HR metrics, you will find that there are a ton of metrics that you could measure. I have a bias toward measuring fewer KPIs (key performance indicators), because too many leads to analysis paralysis. In terms of the Insight Score, you just need to answer two questions: Do I have the right people (to take me to the next level)? Am I confident that I can retain them?

Let's walk through some measures:

Employee happiness: I was the chief product officer at a company called TINYpulse, which is a platform that builds employee engagement technology to determine employee happiness. This is a topic I have spent a lot of time thinking about. Employee satisfaction is an important metric that you should be tracking on a regular basis. The key piece of this metric is to measure it regularly. The annual employee survey is going the way of the dodo bird.

Why is it critical to track this in the context of the Insight Score and this book? The happier your employees are, the more engaged they are. Employee unhappiness is an indicator of employee churn, which can kill your company. Whether you use a tool like TINYpulse or Google Forms, make sure to keep the survey no more than one or two questions. Publish the results so all employees can see them—and be sure to read all the feedback. Discuss the results openly and articulate what you want to do about the key findings. Also, make sure you can look at the data by group. That really helps to identify problem spots.

Retention rate: This is a key indicator of how your organization is retaining its employees. There are two types of employee turnover: voluntary and involuntary. The way that I remember the distinction is by saying to myself: "An employee voluntarily left the business to go someplace else, and another employee was involuntarily let go from the business." I also like to track employees who leave voluntarily and whether the loss was regrettable or not regrettable—not everyone that leaves your business is regrettable, but you want to make sure you do not lose your high-potential employees.

Make sure to track this data by manager as well. Sometimes you can find the good managers versus the bad managers if there's a trend line of highly regrettable employee losses. Of course, it could also be a concern outside of the manager's control, like the fact that a job type is in high demand, which means you should be looking at your compensation guidelines. The point is to track it and make the insights actionable.

In any business, finding the right talent is expensive, and finding new talent to replace them is equally expensive.

One last comment—calculate your employee churn by hire date, so that you can look at your retention rate by cohorts. For example, are you losing new hires, or are they long-tenured employees?

Financial efficiency: There's a panoply of data on this topic. I like to look at revenue per full-time employee and EBITDA by full-time employee. I follow these metrics over time to see how the numbers are trending. I also like to understand the benchmarks from other competitors or similar businesses. There are many ways to get this data, especially if you are comparing yourself to public companies. Heck, you can also cobble together your own view by using resources like LinkedIn as a proxy.

In the technology sector, you typically want to see a business with at least $200,000 in revenue per employee. Some of the best-run tech businesses are over $1 million per employee; Netflix and Apple are around $2 million. EBITDA per employee can be all over the map, and having a reference point is important. If you are in reinvestment mode, you will likely not have much, if any, EBITDA per employee.

These metrics are great to track because they help you understand a bit about the health of your team. They will bring up interesting questions, like: Are you reinvesting in the business enough? Are you extracting more profit versus other competitors in the space, or are you less efficient?

You could continue to go *crazy* with HR metrics. But in the context of your Insight Score, you want to have a sense of whether you have a healthy, talented, and retained team. Of course, this does not address whether you have the *right* team. So let's get into that now.

Organizational Future State

This is the process I have used in various companies, most recently at Rosetta Stone. You can do it across your entire company. I will walk through how I approach this with key management.

If you have done the work throughout this book and have a sense of where you are going (your vision) and whether you are feeding the existing business or moving to another one (or somewhere in between), I always recommend building a future state of what your organization should look like in terms of the roles and aptitude you will need and how it could look in the future. If you spend an enormous amount of time building annual and multiyear plans, why wouldn't you also do the work to think about what the future structure and team should look like to support the business? Don't put current people in those spots, though, because a whole host of biases will enter into your decision-making and thought processes.

I don't like to get fancy with these exercises. You can use a ton of online tools: Google Docs, Microsoft Word, etc.— whatever works for you! I am asking you to draw boxes. Yes, boxes (details below). You will be surprised how hard it is, because you have to make decisions on areas to beef up or maybe reduce. You have to think about the types of new team members you need to attract or how you will grow current team members into your next stage of growth.

Reviewing Talent Depth: Is It the Right Team (for Where You Are Going)?

Once you understand what the future state of your organization should look like, then you should dig into the detail of the types of team members you have today. It's super important to do the hard work on your people analysis when you are considering how confident you are that you have the right team in place to unlock value in your company—and if you don't, then you'd better figure out a plan to get there.

When you are looking at making a leap to the next box as a market-leading star, you need to know whether you have the right team or not. This is especially important if you pivot into a different business that requires different skill sets, and/or the scale of your business now requires different skill sets. The chart below, which I call the virtuous cycle of talent management, will help you with this review. Let's go through it in some detail, with some diagram examples:

The Virtuous Cycle of Talent Management

MELISSA YATES MAY, 2020

Identification of critical roles: After you have done the future-state organization, you might notice that you have some holes, such as skills or roles that you don't have, etc. Start by writing down all the skills and capabilities you need. For instance, perhaps you need to upgrade your sales leader because your current head of sales is lacking analytical skills. They have not built a strong sales operational capability within the organization and aren't interested in doing that. Create a simple job description and the attributes that you would want or need to fill that gap. (It's totally OK if your team is perfect, too. In that case, consider yourself lucky!)

Nine-box assessment: The nine-box process is an oldie but a goodie. It's a great way to evaluate your current team. You basically plot them on a nine-box chart, as shown below.

The GE-McKinsey Nine-Box Matrix

Potential: The ability to assume increasingly broad or complex roles as business needs change.

	Developing	Achieving	Surpassing
High Potential	**Rough Diamond** — Develop	**Solid Star** — Stretch/ Develop	**Future Leader** — Stretch/ Promote
Medium Potential	**Yellow Flag** — Observe/ Exit	**Solid Talent** — Develop	**Rising Star** — Stretch/ Develop
Limited Potential	**Red Flag** — Exit	**Steady Talent** — Observe/ Develop	**Master/ Mentor** — Hold/ Develop

Performance (based on current job): The extent to which the individual:
a) Delivers business/functional results
b) Demonstrates core competencies
c) Acts in the spirit of the company's values

MCKINSEY & COMPANY

I find that the nine-box model is powerful because of its simplicity and effectiveness. You plot "potential" and "performance" on a grid, with performance measured along the x-axis and potential along the y-axis. The most valuable position is the top right box. That person would be the highest-ranking in both performance and potential.

You should use the nine-box model for succession planning and to evaluate talent in your organization. This is literally one of those times that I like being "inside the box." It forces me to make decisions and action plans on talent. When you assess your employees, it's important to understand what "performance" and "potential" are in this context. The "performance level" is what the employee does and how they do it. The "potential level" is what the employee is capable of attaining. Think of this as their raw ability, motivation to succeed, and commitment to the group or organization. Simply said, potential is the assessment of an employee's ability to rise and to succeed in a more senior or expanded role; performance is how they are working and what they are delivering today.

At any stage of growth, you need to have a successor in mind, or have a path to having one. This mentality should continue throughout the organization. If you're a startup leader, have an honest conversation with yourself about your ability to scale. If you're a leader in a larger company, use this exercise to have regular, open, and honest conversations about succession and performance as part of your annual performance planning as well as your quarterly check-ins.

Skill-gap analysis and readiness assessment: After you have evaluated your team(s), you should have a list of skills that are consistent for your organization and that should be worked on. Look at your team, and determine any gaps in these key areas. As the manager and leader, you should be allocating your time to determining development actions that need to be taken to enable their growth.

Perform a skill-gap analysis. Pay special attention to each team member's "time to readiness"—how long will it take to develop this person? Readiness is a tricky topic. Every good coach or manager does a good job of highlighting areas of improvement in isolated sets of development practice. I am not a golfer, but I have always wanted to be. In the last year, I have taken two lessons. The first lesson had the instructor literally giving me four or five things to work on within the span of five minutes. There was no way that I could get enough reps on all those things in one lesson to see an improvement. The other lesson had the instructor walking me through one thing to focus on for the entire lesson, which I was much more able to do. The improvement was clear, and I was happy that I could see it right away.

Readiness is one of those areas where I think it's wise to find one or two areas of development. It's an obvious red flag if one of your key lieutenants has a tremendous amount of work to do across all the skills. Some of the skills that are easier to approach are obtaining more experience and specialized skills. You can focus on giving that team member more challenging tasks or special projects, or you can invest in education or certificate programs for them. The harder skills to solve are things like "initiative." You can expose the team member to tasks as small as running a key business review every month, so they get experience leading a meeting, or something larger, like leading an acquisition. However, I have found that some team members just don't have that initiative gene. They are hard-wired not to have it.

I would like to stress a very important point. As you look to unlock the value in your company, it's also your job to unlock the value in your employees. Just because you need to upgrade a team member doesn't mean that they don't have or add value. Your job as a leader is to cultivate your team's potential so that they are better off after they have moved on to a different company or a different role.

Development planning: Lastly, have a development plan. But have your team member draft and devise their own plan. If you can afford it, have the employee seek help from an executive coach. But the key is to have a plan so that the skills gaps are being addressed and you are their accountability partner. I have done this process many times, and it becomes even more powerful if you are willing to share your development plan with a wider group of people. The key is to have an active plan so that you can develop your people as your business grows.

Another way you can help is to introduce "stop/start/keep doing" surveys with your team. You literally ask your teams what each team member should start doing, stop doing, and keep doing. Use this practice to better provide feedback and to keep the process of skill-gap analysis on track. This is just good management.

The worst thing you can do as a leader is not have open and honest conversations—especially if everyone's aligned on being a market leader. For example, I once took on a role in a startup that was run by a good friend of mine. I was on the board, and the board asked me to replace the CEO, who also happened to be my friend. Looking back on this experience, I don't believe the board gave my friend adequate feedback— the decision felt rushed and a bit knee-jerk. It was a difficult situation, but our friendship endured. He continued on with the company, running product for a while, and then he took on a larger role at Amazon.

The key point is that you do not want to surprise someone. Help your team members grow, and cultivate a culture
of learning.

Final Word

If you could wave your magic wand, you would love to have
the best talent at every position. The best way to have an
awesome team is to hire the smartest people and grow them
along with your graph. But that's not always possible. Reed
Hastings, in his book *No Rules Rules: Netflix and the Culture of
Reinvention*, discussed his belief that having "talent density
in the most important roles is one of the keys to Netflix's success." His book is chock-full of solid advice. On the surface
it seems simple: Hire the best people, then build a culture of
performance with radical candor and feedback.

Of course, Netflix is a market leader. They have a significant competitive advantage in the market that they have built
over time. To take your business to the next level, you need a
culture that is hyper-focused on performance management,
and you will need to pay the highest compensation for that
talent. If you are of the mindset that you cannot afford the
best talent, I would suggest thinking about having a wider
aperture on where you find talent.

These days, you can find talent everywhere. Since the pandemic, remote work is even more of a reality; employers are
more open to it, and it can be a real advantage to companies.
While compensation is an important piece of the employ-
ment puzzle, if you can tap into the core drivers of motivation
for your company and team, you can build a company that
endures and that can become special. In his 2009 book *Drive*,
New York Times–bestselling author Daniel Pink writes about
tapping into our intrinsic motivation. He describes the three

elements of the motivation formula: autonomy, mastery, and purpose. The companies that figure out how to tap into their teams' intrinsic motivation in this new age of remote work are going to have an incredible advantage.

I believe you can find talent everywhere due to the COVID-19 macro trend. You can have contractors, you can have a fractional workforce, you can find talent in developing countries—you can find talent anywhere. I believe that work from home and hybrid home/office environments are here to stay, and that you can find a density of talent anywhere. For instance, Rosetta Stone uses an outsourced mobile software development firm in Croatia. Their work is fantastic.

Based on this data, you have some decisions to make. You need to put in the time cultivating and growing people. That is more than just doing a one-on-one and asking your employee how their weekend was. You need to hold yourself accountable to building out your team and how that team should and can develop over time. This needs to be a discussion with your co-founders, partners, board, etc. Having a thoughtful plan on how you want to build out your team enables everyone to also understand your plans for career development.

Evaluating Diversity

Diversity, equity, and inclusion (DE&I) is getting more and more attention in the corporate world, which is absolutely right from a moral and social justice perspective. If you are the living embodiment of Ebenezer Scrooge, then it's also just good for business. Global consulting firm McKinsey did a 2015 study called "Why Diversity Matters." The net finding was that companies in the top quartile of gender diversity were 15 percent more likely to produce above-average profitability. It also showed that diverse companies had 19 percent higher revenue than non-diverse companies. This just makes social and business sense, since a more diverse company means more diverse perspectives and greater innovation.

This subject is very deep and has a lot of different elements to it. At the end of the day, you will have to decide on your own DE&I approach based on your culture and values. But it's absolutely obvious that unlocking your company's value has to include a diverse team. Here are a couple of ideas to kickstart your thinking:

Start with the top of the funnel: Your recruiting needs to be as inclusive as possible. It's common to get all of your hires from your own network, and the system of job referrals is fantastic in that the potential employee is a known entity, which could mean higher performance. However, referrals tend to look like the referrer. If you are a white manager, the odds are that your professional network looks like you. A few tips to avoid this:

Blind résumés: Have your recruitment efforts remove text and images that would hint at age, race, ethnicity, etc. Trust me: we all have biases, and if you have one minute to look at a résumé, you will undoubtedly bring in some of yours.

Demand diverse hiring: Demand that a certain percentage of your hires come from whatever talent pools you are focused on as part of your DE&I culture. Your hiring managers may be upset because there will be a perception that the company is "slowing down" the hiring process. That could be true. However, you should push your teams to have a company-specific dictated representation of candidates in your hiring funnel. It's hard to change the diversity of your team if you don't first tackle the inbound recruitment process.

Consistent hiring practices: You need to interview everyone the same way. Create a standard set of questions or a question bank for all applications. Whether you use a fancy ATS (application tracking system) or a spreadsheet, make sure that everyone asks the same questions to each candidate. This is a good practice overall, since over time, you will be able to see trends in how different interviewees answer questions.

Find talent in unexpected places: Try to align yourself with hiring sources from diverse talent pools. This can be formal or informal. I personally support the organization Year Up, which focuses on helping socially disadvantaged youth. There are a ton of organizations that you can partner with. You can recruit from places like HBCUs (historically black colleges and universities) or diverse special interest groups. You can also just reach out to a professional in your field who you respect and who has a diverse network. The point is that "finding diverse talent is difficult" is not an acceptable excuse.

Have diversity KPIs: What you track becomes your reality. You should be public with your goals regarding diversity and get as specific as possible. If you want to have more leadership that is diverse, make a commitment to this, and track your progress. Otherwise, your efforts can be viewed as hollow.

Career development: Make active efforts to find opportunities for diverse talent to work on special projects and get access to key leadership. The more sponsorship you do across your organization, the more likely you will be to break the trend of privileged groups getting all the best opportunities.

Be public about your efforts: Your inside efforts embracing DE&I should be authentic—and once you have built a system that supports your organization's values, you should be aggressive in communicating your commitment publicly on your own website, as well as on sites such as Glassdoor. This will also attract more diverse talent.

I am an optimistic person by nature. And I think the discussions we're having regarding DE&I are super healthy and long overdue. We can all do better—and do this faster—as business leaders. But I'm hopeful that we are now starting to see more diversity in the boardroom and across leadership teams globally.

Diversity in Your Products

Just like we mentioned in above, diversity in the workplace still has a ways to go. Just as important as diversity in your teams is building diversity into your products. If you think about it, how can you have product diversity if you don't have a diverse team? A survey of design industry demographics (the 2019 Design Census) found that almost three-quarters of designers, 71 percent, identified as white, while 9 percent were Asian and 8 percent were Hispanic. Only 3 percent were black. This sort of skewed ethnicity representation is not uncommon in the technology sector.

At Rosetta Stone, we actually codified our standards for "diversity by design." Obviously, Rosetta Stone is an iconic brand that has a global audience. It's paramount that the company do the best possible job of representing its global audience in its products. We worked hard to build diversity into our consciousness and to think about it every day—to the point where diversity by design was just a part of every fiber of our business. So how can your company follow a similar path?

Here is an example of the framework that we created at Rosetta Stone, which is a useful set of guidelines for any company to adopt:

Respect and reflect cultural uniqueness. Communicate an appreciation of varied cultures across the globe—for instance, by using inclusionary and welcoming language and images. Reflect your company's values and commitment to diversity while being respectful of others' views. Create learning experiences that are culturally relevant but still broadly approachable by others outside of any specific culture, to the extent possible.

Honor and consider learner uniqueness. Use clear language as much as possible (e.g., to support emerging multilinguals, individuals with disabilities, etc.). Strive to support different learning preferences, goals, and environments in which learners use your products. Consider the principles of universal design, and integrate accessible design thinking as you create and communicate about your products.

Be conscious of bias, and continuously work to overcome it in the design of your products and services. Invite expanded knowledge and awareness of customer diversity. Engage in regular training on topics such as anti-bias education and unconscious bias, and promote open communication. Have a willingness to learn from your customers, community, and colleagues. Maintain diverse feedback loops that inform the creation of future products, media, and services.

Avoid creating a social context of in-groups and out-groups. Do not resort to using stereotypes based on age, class, race, ethnicity, sexual orientation, gender identity, religion, beliefs, geography, or physical ability. Do not employ tokenism. Do not use exclusionary or loaded language. Do not design learning that privileges one group or harms others.

An example of how we put this approach into practice at Rosetta Stone was a product we introduced called Rosetta Stone English, which adopts an asset model that focuses on what students can do—their strengths, skills, talents, interests, and competencies. Learners' backgrounds, heritage languages, and cultures are celebrated as assets, not deficits. For this reason, learners are described as "emerging multilinguals" rather than "English-language learners," acknowledging that by learning English, they will become bilingual/multilingual.

No company is perfect, and we should all be striving to do better. Having both a diverse team and codified principles to execute on product design ensures that your company is intentional and thoughtful about building products that truly reflect the world around us.

Diversity of Personality

It's extremely valuable to have different perspectives that include diversity of gender, ethnicity, and sexual orientation—but also diversity of thought. If you build out a team that looks and acts exactly like you, you will get exactly that type of company.

There are many examples of how this has worked out really well for some companies. I think of the early days of Microsoft, where every Microsoft person I had a meeting with felt like a mini replica of Bill Gates: smart, hard-charging, tenacious, and sometimes very rude.

I would always advocate for a more balanced team. Do you want to have a team that approaches every situation the same way? I don't think so. I remember the series many years ago called *Star Trek: The Next Generation*. The incredible character played by Patrick Stewart oversaw a perfectly balanced team. You had a Klingon who usually wanted to attack a problem (literally), and then the ship's counselor advocating for talking through the situation to get everyone's perspective.

Stewart's character, Captain Jean-Luc Picard, would listen to all the feedback from the team and then make a decision. I wish all my staff meetings ran like that.

When building out your team, I believe that personality assessments can better help you to manage, collaborate, and build out very balanced teams. I have used the Emergenetics personality test with a lot of success. Another popular approach is DISC, which stands for the four main personality profiles described in the assessment model: dominance, influence, steadiness, and conscientiousness. The main criteria represent the following personality types:

Dominant: These team members are "task-oriented." People with D personalities tend to be confident and decisive, and they value the importance of accomplishing bottom-line results. They represent 10 percent of the population.

Inspiring: These team members are more "people-oriented." They tend to be communicative and place an emphasis on relationships. They are usually the most outgoing team members, and they seek to persuade or influence others. This personality type encompasses about 25 to 30 percent of the population.

Supportive: These team members are people-oriented too, but they are also more reserved. They tend to be dependable and place the emphasis on cooperation and stability. They represent 30 to 35 percent of the population.

Cautious: These team members are task-oriented and more reserved. They are really focused on quality and accuracy. They make up about 20 to 25 percent of the population.

The reality is that we do act differently based on the personality of the person we are working with, the situation, and, frankly, how the other person behaves. The DISC (or Emergenetics) assessment does a nice job of capturing some of these details, and I believe it's helpful. For instance, when I run meetings, I tend to reflect on the different personality sensibilities of each team member. I find that it's also helpful to show the work product of these tests to your team from time to time. I would also recommend spending some time on a regular basis, perhaps at your annual planning meeting, talking to your employees about the makeup of your team around diversity of thought.

I think back to my team at Rosetta Stone. We were heavily directive and control focused. In fact, our nickname was the "Action Team." When we rebuilt Rosetta Stone, we were looking for more action-oriented, execution-oriented management team members. We were a small-cap public company, and investors wanted returns (fast). We didn't have time to be contemplative, and we knew what we wanted to do. So we were intentional about building a team that was very aggressive and chock-full of seasoned, competent managers. That team fit that mandate, but another company and another mandate would be better off with a completely different team.

I have been working with Judy Goldberg as my executive coach for years. She is the founder of Wondershift LLC, which she describes as "a firm focused on results-driven transformation, helping leaders to shift their businesses and employees to be more successful, productive, strategic, and present." Here are her thoughts on the value of embracing cognitive diversity:

How have you used personality assessments (communication assessment tools) when working with leadership teams?

Leaders, like all humans, think and behave differently. By using assessments, my goal is to create a platform that provides a new and easily understandable lens for leaders to recognize the power of cognitive diversity (diversity of thought) and how it impacts their approach to developing solutions, exploring ideas, and embracing opportunities.

Though there are many great assessments out there, I mostly use Emergenetics, and my clients love it, so I am sticking with it for now. It's a multifaceted tool for understanding human behavior and the unique differences in the way people approach work and life.

I use these assessments in hopes that leadership teams will take a pause from their go-go-go schedules and truly listen and learn from one another, so that they can move away from groupthink and into healthy debate and meaningful discussions. When teams are designed with cognitive diversity in mind, I have witnessed greater productivity, faster and more effective problem solving, better meeting [of] the needs of their clients and customers, and [businesses] achieving an overall more inclusive and civil environment for all.

What are the best practices on how to use the data and insights from this process?

Accountability: Pair up team members who think differently from each other to act as opposite profile advisors. Encourage these pairs to communicate with their differing preferences on different topics. They can bounce ideas off each other, send draft communications to one another to review, and even role-play. This accountability will teach people to assume positive intent. It's a mindset shift that takes some work. Instead of stepping into someone's shoes, they can step into one another's minds.

Communication audit: Review emails, team communications, company-wide keynotes—ask yourself if you are writing from your personal preference and perspective or creating a whole-brain communication that will be received well by all.

Share and compare: The more open people are to share prefer-ences, the more we can learn about one another. It takes two to tango, as the old saying goes, so both people may need to flex preferences to get the most out of a conversation.

Diversifying your team: As your team evolves, in addition to considering performance and potential, you also must con-sider every aspect of diversity, including cognitive diversity and neurodiversity, when building a team. You are inevitably going to want to have team members who are very different from you—those who will be able to see things that you can't, challenge you, and overall make your decisions better.

What are the common issues that you see when working with leadership teams?

I am often asked, "Can you help me work with this difficult person? Communicating with them is so hard." My response is always the same: "Who is the difficult one?" At times this brings a little nervous laughter, and I go on to say, "Is it that they are difficult or could they just be different?"

It's human nature to sync up and naturally be attracted to those who "get you," because these are the people where things just seem to flow. You can easily communicate with them, and they may have a similar way of approaching the world.

On the flip side, I recently heard the phrase, "If it doesn't 'fit,' it's not legit." Imagine all the times someone who didn't "fit" or had a different view or approach was judged, reacted to negatively, or even dismissed. This could get dangerous!

Leadership teams need to be aware of when they are shutting someone or something down too soon or throwing out an idea that seems off the norm before even exploring it. This unique piece of knowledge or perspective could be the game changer.

To grow, I firmly believe leaders must be able to hold two opposing ideas in their minds, seek different perspectives, and consider both the intent and impact of their communications, so that what they intend to communicate is what is heard when they deliver a message.

One leader I worked with sent out a global communication with company updates. He focused on the data, the new systems, and the next steps. Though clear, he missed out on communicating the bigger vision of why these changes would benefit the company and employees, and he did not recognize, reward, or mention anyone he worked with along the way. For those with analytical and structural preferences, he hit the mark. Those [who were] more conceptual or relational felt disconnected and deflated.

Leaders need to remember that they have a team of people working for them and with them on achieving a vision. An issue I see is when leadership teams feel they need to develop all the answers. They are missing out on tapping into the diverse brains in the organization.

KEY TAKEAWAYS FROM THIS CHAPTER

Your team can be a major accelerator if you have determined that your ability to unlock value in your company is high and you have a shot at being a market leader. Taking the time to evaluate your team against the journey and growth path that you want to take is an important part of evaluating how much momentum you can generate. The questions are tough: What talent do I need for the next stage of growth? How should my business be structured to support that momentum?

Here are some key highlights from this chapter. Using your team to build momentum is a process where you do the following:

- Evaluate your team using the nine-box matrix to determine their current performance and future potential. Conduct a skill-gap analysis to determine any gaps related to competencies, skills, experience, and education as defined for a particular role. You have already identified the skills you need from the first step. Make sure to build development plans to help you close any skills gaps.

- Create a system of diversity that incorporates inclusive hiring and interview processes and the evaluation of diversity outcomes.

- Build diversity by design into everything you do. Ensure that you are incorporating cultural and social principles in all aspects of your product design and creation.

- Understand your team's personality diversity so that you can have a team that is not only action-oriented but also long-term oriented and thoughtful about the future, as this will support your company's growth goals.

10

USING CAPITAL TO INCREASE YOUR MOMENTUM

THROUGHOUT THIS BOOK I've told stories of existing legacy companies as well as startups. To be honest, it's been a struggle to offer equally great advice to business leaders who are at all these different stages. This chapter focuses heavily on venture capital–based financing—that early-stage, very risky financing where the chances of success are limited, but success will bring transformational outcomes.

I toyed with taking this section out of the book, but I decided that my personal-investing pitch style might work for you. So if you're a business leader working for an established business, you can skip this chapter.

If you are still reading, this chapter provides a cursory example of the common financing mechanisms for most companies, both public and private. I would highly recommend Brad Feld's book on raising capital, *Venture Deals: Be Smarter Than Your Lawyer and Venture Capitalist*. Brad is a phenomenal teacher and investor. I almost partnered with him years ago on an early-stage idea, and I have to say that he was both wicked smart and incredibly kind. His book is approachable for any audience.

As I said earlier, not only is it your job as the leader of a business to not run out of money; in the context of the Insight Score, you also need to be able to raise the right amount of capital to finance your growth. Whether they are big or small, most companies use a combination of debt and equity to finance their growth. The number of financial instruments, bankers, and options for this section are so vast, I don't even want to go there in this book. Trust me when I say that there's a plethora of ways to find financing with an infinite number of good choices for you as the business owner. You just need to make sure that you have a good business, a business plan, or cash flow from one of your businesses to have a solid venture.

Bootstrapping: You can actually do this form of financing as a public or private company. In essence, bootstrapping is using your own cash or personal finances for your business. If you are an entrepreneur, you are very familiar with this line of financing. It's your cash, your friends' and family's cash, or your credit cards. If you are an established company, you are using your own cash or the cash of another business to finance another investment. This form of financing typically enables you to retain more control of your business as an entrepreneur or as a public company (or doesn't dilute your current investors). You will have to decide for yourself on the trade-offs you want to make—the main trade-off being how much of the business you want to retain versus not growing fast enough to pursue an opportunity due to potentially not deploying enough capital.

Debt: There are a ton of options with debt. When interest rates are low, make sure to get debt. With debt you are not giving away a piece of your business like you are with equity. The level of debt depends on the business and your ability to repay it.

Venture capital: A venture capital (vc) investment is a form of private equity that primarily focuses on investments in startups and small businesses. These investments are typically made when the business has little to no real revenue traction. This is considered a riskier asset class because the investments have a high rate of failure, especially with earlier investments. Venture capitalists look to place bets across many types of early-stage businesses because of the variability of returns. vcs sometimes specialize by a business vertical (e.g., health care, technology, energy) or by the size of the investment (or the size of the check they write). Early stages are typically called "seed" deals and can range from small to very large investments. Later-stage investments are less risky to investors. The later the stage, the bigger the check and the lower the returns. For early-stage companies, the inverse is true because of the increased risk.

Private equity: A similar but different notion to venture capital is private equity, except the return profile is different and varied. PE firms are looking for more predictable returns from existing businesses where they either purchase the whole company or a portion of the company. A PE firm can perform what is called a leveraged buyout, which means it buys a company (typically public) using very little cash by using debt to finance most of the transaction. The firm looks to hold the asset for three to five years and then sell it to another PE firm or another company, or they might take the asset public through an initial public offering. PE firms can also inject growth capital into private companies where they own a piece (typically a majority) of the company.

Public company fundraising: You can have a field day with different ways to raise money in the capital markets. Being a public company has its pain; there are tons of regulatory and compliance costs. It can also force management teams to be extremely short-sighted by focusing on quarterly results. However, there are pluses. You can finance acquisitions through your own stock, and you can also raise more money through a secondary stock offering. This can be dilutive or non-dilutive. If an existing investor sells existing shares to other investors, then it's non-dilutive. If the investor issues more shares to new investors, then current investors get diluted (or own less of a share of the company). Another instrument is a private investment in public equity (PIPE). This is similar to a secondary offering, but it has some differences. It allows an investor to buy shares in public company stock below its market value. There are some advantages to this mode of financing, primarily fewer regulatory requirements. However, the discounted price does dilute current investors.

When to raise money and how much you should raise (if you need it) are important questions that this book does not answer. However, the makings of that answer are in your business planning. For example, if you have product/market fit; your customers are salivating at the mouth from using your product (meaning it's highly engaging and you are getting renewals, positive word of mouth, etc.); and you have a thoughtful plan to grow the demand in your product, then you have the answer to the "use of proceeds" for your capital raise, in case you don't have the capital to self-fund it.

There are so many books and blogs on this topic. But I will say this: If you believe you're going to be one of the special companies that can grow and have huge returns, then I'd raise as much money as I possibly could at the best valuation. You cannot predict when capital markets will turn negative. I'll never forget the time my business partner and I closed a $20 million round of financing with Sequoia Capital and other blue-chip investors in the early 2000s—right before the Web 1.0 bubble burst (for the younger readers, this was an epic stock market crash). The company survived this economic nuclear winter to eventually have a so-so exit—but it was very close. In another example, I closed a round of financing with Draper Fisher Jurvetson right before the next huge market crash, in 2008. I must have a thing for timing right before market implosions. The point is that you obviously need enough capital to fuel your existing or new venture. Always have enough gas in your capital tank.

If you are a private company deciding whether to take outside investment for the first time, remember this: once you take outside investment, the fundraising never stops until you have a liquidity event. When you take equity investment from an outside party, you lose a little bit of control over your business. If you believe you're going to be one of those market leaders making billions of dollars, then it would be the right call to own a small portion of that business versus trying to retain a larger stake of a smaller business. You certainly want to think hard before giving up control of your company and the conditions under which to do so. But in general, raise big early. Raise when you're at your strongest—when you have strong revenue growth, a great team, traction in the market, etc.

Determine How Much Capital to Raise and When

Capital allocation is the most important piece of a CEO's job. In fact, if you have not already read it, I would recommend William N. Thorndike Jr.'s book *The Outsiders: Eight Unconventional CEOs and Their Radically Rational Blueprint for Success*. It's a literary master class in capital allocation.

Don't obsess too much on the instruments of raising capital. There are tons of bankers and investment professionals you can hire to help you. There are also a ton of financial professionals. You can shake a tree and find consultants to help you with financial planning. But the question you should be focused on is: What and where is the best use of my capital? Hopefully you have a sense by now that T3PM walks you through this process.

Whether you're a private or public company, I wanted to jot down some of my golden rules for capital requirements:

Have at least twelve months of operating cash. Always have enough in the tank. I've been in many situations as a startup where I almost couldn't make payroll. This is not fun or exciting. You will not be in the driver's seat of your business if you don't have options. If you are running out of money, investors will want their capital back in some form, or your valuation gets diluted, or investors look for opportunities to screw with you, or all the above. Again, this is not fun—avoid this situation by all means necessary.

Understand capital allocation. Understand where your dollars go to the highest return. There are some great frameworks out there. For example, in the SaaS space, a common framework is called the "rule of forty." Simply put, if your growth rate minus your EBITDA is at least forty, then you are performing appropriately. I use a simple framework that evaluates whether you are growing appropriately based on whether you are a *growth*, *optimize*, or *harvest* business. For instance, if you are a growth company but not growing as fast as the market, then you should be asking yourself, "Why not?" Conversely, if you are growing a business to harvest it, which means you are not able to grow it because it's long in the tooth, then you should be able to keep margins high since you are sustaining the business. You don't want to be in a growth business that is not exceeding market share growth or a harvest business that does not have expanding margins. This is shockingly obvious, but you would be surprised how many companies have a hard time confronting the realities of their business performance.

If you already have an existing business or product, you can always take cash from one business and give it to the other. You can perform your own analysis internally to decide where there's an opportunity to allocate your capital. For example, at Rosetta Stone, my business (the language business) was deemed to be more of a harvest business when I first joined the company, so we used its cash flow to fund our faster-growing literacy division. That was the right choice for investors then; later we made the decision to take the company private to unlock more value across all of our businesses.

Be clear about your planned use of proceeds. Whether you are trying to fund your business or project internally or externally, you must be clear about what you will do with the capital proceeds. I have seen so many crappy "ask" presentations where the use of proceeds is not clear. Have a business plan where you can walk through your assumptions and your specific areas of investment. The plan should be detailed. For instance, if you need capital to increase demand via variable marketing, then walk through the specific channels you are going to invest in and how that demand converts into customers.

Set up stage gates. Many investments are what a former colleague would have called "heaven on whiteboard." Simply
put, you can make anything successful in a spreadsheet. I
always advise setting up "stage gates." These are a predefined
set of hurdles to determine if your investment idea has merit.
For example, you can put a stage gate around an early product idea or a large investment in a marketing campaign. This
enables the entrepreneurs and operators to self-define what
success looks like and obtain autonomy, while enabling management and investors some level of governance. I am sure
you have had experience with a project that has gone out of
control—teams building bloated products that no one wants
or ideas that just don't work. Stage gates will help you avoid
these nightmare scenarios.

Before you roll your eyes (if you are an early-stage startup
founder), I am just talking about being agile. If you think
about it, it makes a lot of sense to divide an initiative into
separate "chunks." At each stage gate, you look to see if the
thing is working and then add more capital if it hits your own
success criteria.

Tips on Raising Money

Amazon has an internal process—when they build products,
they write a future-state press release of what the launch
should look like. The collaboration SaaS company Atlassian has a similar process for their product teams that they
call "build a box." The teams decorate a mock product (in
the shape of a cereal box) and construct the key benefits and
positioning as if they were the marketing team for a consumer goods company. I like to perform a similar process with

companies that is related to their future capital needs. Even if you don't plan to raise money, it gives you a perspective on what this business looks like. It'll include much of what you have already thought through in this book.

There are no half measures in business—unless you just have a shitty business. You are either going to do it or not do it. Just like Yoda says, "There is no try." There is only do or not do—the choice is yours.

The one thing I would say about raising money is that everyone has heard the same investor pitch. There are so many good pitch resources that are publicly available, it will be hard for me to tell you something you haven't heard before. But I will attempt to do so below. In fact, one of my favorite pieces of advice about strutting a pitch deck is from early Apple executive and technology evangelist Guy Kawasaki. Guy has a process called the 10/20/30 rule. His advice is to have no more than ten slides with no more than twenty minutes of presentation time, and the presentation should be in thirty-point font. There are so many startup accelerators, studios, free resources, etc., to help you get a ton more detail—and most importantly, find your own style. Let me repeat that: *find your own style.* I get so tired of hearing the same boring presentations from Y Combinator alumni that I long for a pitch that is a bit different.

I always advise anyone who is pitching to stand out in a crowd. I believe that you always want to leave the room with two things having taken place: Everyone understands your proposition so they can decide whether it's the right investment, and you've left a positive, lasting impression. For example, the last time I raised venture capital was several years ago. At the time I was in my late forties, and the concept was a fan platform using AI in the e-sports space. Everyone in this vertical tends to be in their teens or early twenties, and the implicit uniform starts with wearing a hoodie. Imagine what I looked like pitching investors. To stick out and establish credibility with the concept, I played up my comic book hobby. It wasn't my idea: Greg Gottesman, a partner at Pioneer Square Labs in Seattle, really encouraged me to show my quirkiness in a pitch. So I included a picture of myself dressed in a Batman suit in my office—and yes, I did turn to investors and say, "I am Batman," complete with that dire and grizzly Michael Keaton–style voice. That addressed the stage- and age-appropriate question that might have been an objection in the geeky video gaming business. This approach worked— and it was a helluva lot of fun.

This is not a book on how to raise venture capital. But I will go through my process and how I like to do it, along with my basic structure of how I raise money. This doesn't just apply to startups; many of these principles apply to larger companies as well. Lastly, I would say that you need to be networking with your potential investors at least a year in advance. You can't build a partnership by spamming somebody you don't have a relationship with. You have to be strategically focused on who you want to be working with on the investor front.

This flow is biased toward a private company seeking venture capital, but you can tweak the content based on your own needs. If you have followed all the steps in this book, you should already have the data required to execute on a fantastic investor deck. Let's get down to it.

Executive Summary Slides

Following your title slide, I recommend that your executive summary slides provide a true snapshot of your entire company in a succinct fashion. This is the fifty-thousand-foot view with only the key information. I have provided a template for your elevator pitch and one for a company snapshot. These can be combined into one slide where appropriate.

On slide 2, I suggest providing the following information:

Summary positioning statement: This can include your company's core value proposition, mission, and/or vision. We already discussed the vision and mission in Chapter 8. Under your positioning statement, add two or three concise points that provide reasons to believe that you can deliver on this vision.

Unique intellectual property: For investors, this is where you are putting your emphasis in terms of your intellectual property "big bet." You will want to think long and hard on where you focus your development resources. This one- or two-bullet section will help answer investors' questions about why your product or solution will have defensibility over your competition and why your solution will have strategic interest in an exit.

High-level projections: You will want to make a quick statement in one or two bullets on some key metrics and projections for your business. You should emphasize any traction that you have today. For instance, if you are a pre-revenue company, then emphasize any data you have from customers. Data like unique users, subscribers, etc., can really be useful. You will also want to mention your annual revenue projection and your Year Three revenue projection here.

I recommend a one-bullet description of the company's business model. It should be as simple as, "Our business model is X, and we make money from Y." Otherwise, your potential investor will be wondering during the entire pitch how you are intending to make money—and they will *not* be focused on what you are presenting.

Executive: Mention your executive experience. If you are a seasoned team, then highlight the obvious things, like your career pedigree, companies you have worked for, etc. If you are a younger team, emphasize your years of experience in any relevant field pertaining to your business. If your junior team has a notable advisor or a board member, this would also be good to note—it will help the investor feel better about investing in you. Lastly, mention any awards the company has won.

Your executive summary slides should answer the question of what your company does and why this opportunity is interesting. Finally, you need to make the investor comfortable with the executive team that will be executing on the mission and vision.

Team

I sometimes move the team slide into the executive summary slide. Obviously, this is not as important when we are talking about an internally funded project. If you have an impressive team, then you can decide to pull that to the beginning if you'd like. It depends on how far along your business is and how mature of an operator you are. Of course, as I previously mentioned, you can show some character in the deck. (You can declare that you are Batman!)

Market Position

This slide should address (actually readdress, since you summarized your solution in the earlier slide) what solution you are providing in the marketplace. Your goal in this slide is to present the following points:

- Define your specific solution. You will want to be sure that potential investors are absolutely clear about what your solution is and what it would do for your customers. This is a common problem for entrepreneurs; they tend to get verbose and don't clearly articulate what it is that they are actually delivering to the marketplace.

- What market pain (problem) is being addressed, and why is your solution needed? Or you can state what the customer pain is, which is an even better approach. For example, "Millions of people today have this problem, and they currently use X. We have developed a solution that is faster, better, and cheaper."

- How big is this market pain? (Note: you will already have this information from the first section on TAM.) Be as explicit as you can in painting a picture for the investor— both in describing the size of the problem and your unique solution for a big market.

Market Share and Total Addressable Market

The market share slide is very important because most institutional investors need you to answer the following questions: Is this opportunity big enough? Can your team fill the need in the market you are addressing? I have provided two common formats. Your slide needs to show what market pain is addressed and what market is being addressed. The key aspect to this slide is that investors are going to be looking for a total addressable market (TAM) that is large enough that the small percentage of market share your company addresses could be an interesting business. If you are presenting an opportunity where, in five years, your $20 million in revenue equates to 50 percent of the TAM, then this is just too small. Investors will typically want you to have a healthy revenue line in five years, equating to single-digit market share.

Tell the story: The graphic implementation should be explicit and should tell a very specific story. The sample slide deck is one execution. Think about showing the overall market, your TAM, and possibly other comparable competitors. You will want to clearly state the starting point, Year One, and what Year Five looks like. When showing the overall market opportunity, build out market segmentation (by demographic, psychographic, SIC code, etc.). Get as granular as possible. Layer in specific detail about segmentation growth rates, if possible.

Lastly, you should be able to articulate why today is the best time to address the market opportunity. The slide should contain as much quantifiable data as possible, to tell the story to the investors and convince them that this is the right moment to invest. Make them feel like the market conditions are ripe to exploit your addressable market—and avoid making them feel they are too early in the opportunity.

Business Momentum and KPIs

This slide should show whatever key performance indicators you might have on your current product or solution. If you are at an early stage, you will not have much to show, so you might want to show early results from customer tests or trials. Key customer testimonials would also be a good complement to this slide. If you have any meaningful data, don't be afraid to show it. This slide shows more traditional metrics for a consumer Internet business. Data on unique users, searches, new

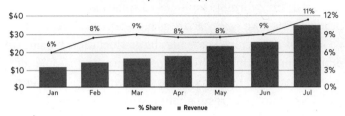

Business Momentum

(Insert your summary statement about the slide)
Give examples of KPIs specific to your business.
Provide commentary here on key points from charts.

versus repeat customers, organic traffic, subscribers, etc., is really useful.

If you are a B2B business, you might want to show your sales funnel here and highlight closed deals (you can also opt to save this information for later in the deck). This data is explicitly telling the investor that your product or service works for your core customers and that there is less risk investing today because there's early traction on the business. Only use this data if it's growing. Showing flat growth trend lines will defeat the goal of this slide.

Product Demos

Investors sometimes clamor to see a demo early in your presentation. You will have to be flexible and determine the ideal time to show a demo. I recommend that you start with your story about your solution and the opportunity. Investors will then be chomping at the bit to see if you have built "real technology." Of course, if you have a real product to show, show it!

I recommend spending half of your pitch time (five to ten minutes) on your demo. The demo should be well prepared and scripted. Show investors your happy path—be intentional about what features you show and the sequence in which you show them. Your demo should reinforce your story. I have provided three formats for you to display examples of your product. Show images that are as high-fidelity as possible to your end-state vision. These may be product shots that are in production or simply high-res mock-ups.

A live demo is best, but if you are giving your pitch virtually, be sure to prepare an alternative. For example, a set of slides that walks through the product could work well as a Plan B in case of connectivity problems. Video walk-throughs may also work as an alternative to a live demo, but make sure that large files are uploaded to cloud platforms before the demo to avoid long delays or clumsy transitions.

I recommend that you prep the devices you will display the product on. Do the following in advance so that you are prepared:

- Turn off any alert-oriented applications like email, push notifications, or instant messaging on all of the devices you will use. These can be extremely annoying to your audience (and potentially embarrassing for you).

- If you are planning a live demo of a mobile product, ensure that you are well practiced at shifting between the demo device (tablet, phone, etc.) and the platform you are using to project the pitch.

- Prepare a clean desktop and home screen by removing any personal background images or arrays of icons.

- Have your demo scripts or files organized and ready to go in one folder that is easy to find and access. I find preloading pages in different tabs works extremely well to avoid slow-loading pages.

- Download any cloud-based docs so that you can easily reference them if a backup is needed.

Your demonstration should be constructed to reinforce the one key point that you made in slides 2 to 4. You will only want to show features that reinforce your points on unique technology or attractiveness to the audience in your TAM. Layer specific examples in the demonstration. These can be comments and feedback from customers or specific pieces of data you have (e.g., the feature is so compelling that customers spend fifteen minutes on this one screen).

Unique IP Slide

This is where you talk about your secret sauce. The investor has already been blown away by your demo. Now you get to explain at a very high level how it works. If you are doing your investor presentations with a technical leader (e.g., the chief technical officer), have that person explain your intellectual property.

You will want to highlight the following:

- Have a simple graphic showing your product or service from a diagram perspective; highlight any patents or patent-pending technology developed in the diagram.

- Your diagram and/or graphic should be very simple; it should be easy enough to understand that a nontechnical investor can follow along.

- Highlight anything in your solution that is unique versus the competition or the market in general. You will want to have three to four points on this topic. Investors are going to want to know how a startup is going to compete against the balance sheet of a much larger company that is better financed.

Competition

Any company that says they don't have competition is not telling the truth. If you don't, the market you are addressing must be so inconsequential that no one wants to be in it. Be prepared to talk about your competitors. An example is below.

Competition

(Insert your summary statement about the slide)

KEY FACTORS	COMPETITOR A	COMPETITOR B	COMPETITOR C
Factor 1	◯	◑	◯
Factor 2	◔	◔	◔
Factor 3	◐	●	◐
Factor 4	◕	◑	◕
Factor 5	●	◯	●

Highlight opportunities specific to your business.

Having as much detail as possible will earn you major respect with your potential investors.

In particular, be prepared to answer the following:

- Who are the competitors, and what are their relative strengths and weaknesses?

- How does your service or product compare to the competitors'?

- What is the sustainable competitive advantage that will protect the company from existing or future competitive products?

The competition slide template is meant to illustrate these points in a very simple format. You should be prepared to talk about the top three or four key success factors of your solution versus the competitors', and only focus on those that you know you can win. Put at least two companies at the top of the grid. You should have any detailed quantifiable data as talking points to this slide. If you have detailed information about a competitor's cost model (especially if it's a public company), then make sure to use that. You will want to illustrate by each success factor how your solution provides efficiency, cost, or scale benefits against the competition.

Timeline

This slide is meant to articulate your operational road map. I recommend breaking up the timeline into "innovation" and general company "milestones." This slide should explicitly show investors that you and your team can execute on your mission. In other words, it shows that you have done real work and were thoughtful about how you did it. You want investors to look at this and say, "This team is getting shit done!"

Here are some ideas on what to put in the timeline:

- Key feature releases.

- Key awards or industry recognition.

- Operational metrics layered across the timeline. Examples would be revenue, number of customers, unique users, a large customer win, etc.

Partners

If applicable, list all the specific revenue, supplier, or customer partners you have. A tip: If you do not have a laundry list of partners, show logos of your partners instead. *Big logos sell*—every time.

The "Ask" Slide

We just finished discussing how important it is to define the use of proceeds.

An example on how to show capital allocation is here:

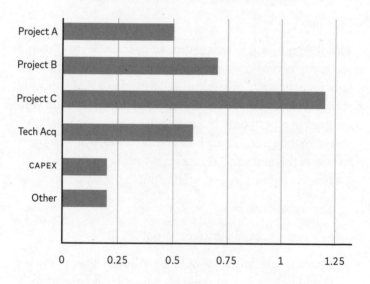

Raising $xM to Accelerate Growth
(Insert your summary statement about the slide)

FINANCING HISTORY	CURRENT RAISE	USE OF PROCEEDS
Insert here	Raising $xM	Summary detail here

In addition, I do not recommend supplying valuation information to potential investors, because you don't want to state a number that is too high or too low. The exception, of course, is if you receive a term sheet with a valuation and you now have the ammunition to "shop" your term sheet to other investors. Of course, if you are a public company and are funding something internally, please ignore this comment.

This slide should provide a basic overview of:

- **Financing history:** Provide details on past investors and the amounts you have received.

- **Current investment amount:** State specifically how much money you are looking to raise.

- **Use of proceeds:** Provide a high-level breakout on how you would use the proceeds of the investment. This should be broken out for things like CAPEX (capital expenditure), labor, contract workers, variable marketing, etc.

Investors are going to assess whether the company is asking for enough money to achieve the next key benchmarks. You should also be prepared to talk about (not in the slide) what a potential exit would be like and from whom. For private investing, you should also be prepared to talk about how many rounds of financing you think your company will need.

Appendix Slides

I recommend that you have two slides as either backup materials or as a soft copy follow-up to investors:

Financial projections and sales model: Financial projections (cash flow and profit and loss) are best made with a one-page spreadsheet showing units shipped, revenue, etc. Projections are typically for three to five years. Investors will not expect the projection for Year Five to be highly accurate. However, the assumptions, detail, and reasonableness for Year One will receive serious examination. You should highlight those key assumptions in a format that is easy to digest. Potential investors expect entrepreneurs to be too optimistic on numbers and are more likely going to want to focus on the underlying assumptions within your model.

Your sales model should show:

- Revenue: Investors prefer bottom-up forecasts supported by real plans. They will consider: What is the timeline of customer interaction to achieve a given revenue assumption? Is the near-term revenue projection supported by the necessary pipeline activity today? How does the long-term projection compare to the total market size? Is the projected share unrealistically high or uninterestingly low?

- Expenses, or the monthly "burn rate" for both the current period and after investment, should be shown.

- Profit before taxes.

- EBITDA.

- Cash flow.

- Capital investment.

- Proceeds from sale of equity.

Some additional notes on this slide: Key assumptions and useful related information should be available on backup slides. Financial projections must be based on more than a one-page spreadsheet. Understanding and implementing the following will be very helpful:

- Having a methodology for developing a financial plan.

- Knowing how to build a credible revenue model.

- Understanding rules for building a usable expense model.

- Having ways to validate the model using publicly available data.

Capitalization table slide: Make sure to supply the details on the total shares outstanding, the ownership stake and absolute number of shares by preferred stockholders (investors), and common shares. You will also want to be explicit on this slide about stating the pre- and post-money valuations for each round of financing.

THERE YOU have it. This is what I have used successfully in the past. Last but not least: Throw in a cool slide or two that shows something about yourself—your unique character traits and quirks. Remember that investors see thousands of pitches. Not everyone shows a picture of themselves dressed up as Batman in their decks.

If you are at a more established company and find my advice to be sophomoric because of your culture or vertical, then I will have to disagree with you. Make sure that you are "appropriate" to your culture, but you can also be unique. For instance, in one of my first board presentations at Rosetta Stone, I showed a slide of the movie poster for the Spaghetti Western classic *The Good, the Bad and the Ugly*. I then proceeded to play the iconic track from that film from composer Ennio Morricone. I did that because I needed to reset the table on the business and felt that a dramatic attention-getter was needed. It got everyone's attention! Most importantly, I was able to get agreement on my change in strategy less than ninety days into the job.

KEY TAKEAWAYS FROM THIS CHAPTER

I'm old-school simple on this. Raise the most money to be
the market leader where you have an advantage (or a high
Insight Score) in business. Allocate capital appropriately
based on expected future returns. And *always* have enough
capital to live through a downturn or catastrophe to fund
your growth when you need it.

Here are some key highlights from this chapter:

* Make the right investment decisions based on what you want
  to do long term. Do the appropriate work on your strategy
  and business planning. Don't worry as much about the suitable financial instrument.

* Have the appropriate plan for funding your business in both
  good times and bad times.

* Have a clear "use of proceeds" so that you understand
  what the expected use of capital is to generate a compelling investor return. Be specific on where you will spend the
  capital, as this gives you a better chance of getting what you
  asked for.

* Build a future-state investor deck that shows you have
  already thought through the investor ask and the key salient
  business points required to raise your capital.

HOW WOULD YOU SCORE THIS SECTION?

You are now ready to make the call on how to score the
"Momentum" question, which is: How confident are you
that you can attract the talent and resources needed to

pull this off? You may be asking yourself, "How should I do this?" since I am guiding you to simultaneously consider two variables: team and capital. Should you weight their importance equally? Is one more important than the other? That's your call. Honestly, if you have high scores across the first four questions, you more than likely won't have a problem with the team. The best talent tends to be attracted to the right opportunities. As long as you have done the work in assessing where your talent needs are today and what they will be in the future, I recommend focusing your time on capital. Capital is the fuel, and your team is the engine. There are no correct answers here. Your determinant is what can accelerate your business, so be honest with yourself on how you score it.

Sometimes, you're in a business that may not be attractive for new capital. Typically, if you are getting higher numbers for the first four questions, you have a business that investors should be interested in, and it will be easier to attract and retain talent.

INSIGHT QUESTION #5

How confident are you that you can attract the talent and resources needed to pull this off?

How to score this question:

- Not at all. (1 pt.)
- Pretty confident. (2 pts.)
- Very. No problem! (3 pts.)

On to the finale!

CONCLUSION
YOUR INSIGHT SCORE

SOCRATES REPORTEDLY once said (because he never wrote shit down) that the "unexamined life is not worth living." Well, I believe that the unexamined business is not worth living. I wrote this book to enable you to continually be examining what you want from your business. Neither you nor your business are on a predetermined path. Where you go is up to you.

We are now at the end of our journey together. I hope you have had a chance to tally up your thoughts through the five key questions.

Think about all those offsite meetings you have attended in your career. I like to create common frameworks that help take the subjectivity out of decision-making while allowing a vast array of inclusive scrutiny over ideas. Hopefully this book accelerates your entire strategic planning process, so you don't have to spend months and/or large sums of money paying a consulting group to do it for you. Instead, do it yourself by distilling your journey down to the five core questions that summarize all you need to determine if you can change your position.

You are ready to assess where you are at with your Insight Score. The math is simple. Multiply the total from questions 1 to 4 by the total from question 5. The higher the score, the better. The floor, where you start to feel confident that you can change your market position, is around 24. If you are near or over 30, get ready to open the champagne, because you should be feeling good about your chances.

As in all frameworks and decision criteria scoring, a lot of this is subjective. The range is a guide; if anything, it should be more instructive about the deeper questions you need to probe, rather than the final arbiter of whether you can unlock value.

As a reminder, here is a guide to what the score tells you about your chances to unlock value:

What Is a Good Insight Score?

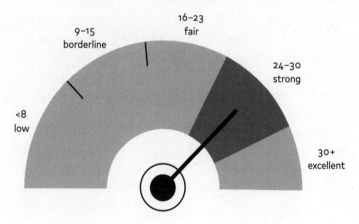

I want to conclude with some sample Insight Scores from my own experience. Not everything I have done has worked out. I have found that when I pursued opportunities in either a subject area that I was not personally passionate about or one I wasn't sure would deliver personal financial gain, those concerns overshadowed the practice of thinking about the practicality of which businesses would be winners or—most germane to this book—had the chance to be winners. Here are a couple of examples on how I would score my ability to use the Insight Score.

Rosetta Stone's Insight Score

I have spent a fair amount of time discussing Rosetta Stone throughout this book. I was brought on to turn around the iconic language business—it had lost its luster. The team and I had a very successful outcome for our employees and investors, as we sold the business and took it private.

When I was recruited, a lot of peers and mentors I am close to really tried to discourage me from taking the role. I remember comments like, "It's a dinosaur," "What a shit show," and my favorite, "Are they still around?" My initial reaction to the business was a strong interest in wanting to give back to society. In fact, it was Rosetta Stone's literacy division (Lexia Learning) that was my biggest draw to the company, since both my son and I suffer from dyslexia, and Lexia's software dramatically improves literacy for young kids and adults.

I also saw Rosetta Stone as an opportunity where I knew I could make a difference, since I have spent a lot of time helping existing businesses perfect their strategies and go-to-market execution. Taking a step back and looking at

Rosetta Stone in late 2017, before we initiated the turnaround work, here is how I looked at the business:

TAM: A huge market (language learning is estimated to be a nearly $50 billion market). Also, we applied a tighter view on our serviceable addressable market (SAM), carving out a premium niche for the business. *Score: 3.*

Timing: Digital language-learning products were growing fast, and we had a product that, while not optimized, was far enough along to take advantage of the timing. We had enough of a web and mobile product open to enhancement that were not completely out of the game. Customers liked the speech-first pedagogy, and the move to more native mobile experiences was a natural for the iconic CD-ROM product the company had pioneered. Also, none of the competition had a large enough lead, so we didn't feel we were too far removed from being competitive. *Score: 3.*

Track Record: We previously had a strong record (but didn't when I started) and had a crazy edge with the most-recognized brand. To be honest, the team, the strategy, and the tech stack were a real mess. But the brand and pedagogy were strong enough that we felt we could move from a B2B business back to our consumer business roots. *Score: 1.*

Plan: But we didn't have a focused plan—we had lots of different strategies, and we were focused on B2B sales, not on our iconic consumer business (the consumer had the larger market and strong brand awareness). The language business didn't really have a cohesive plan or a strong operational structure. The team definitely had a lot of work to do here, hence the low score. *Score: 1.*

And last but not least:

Momentum: We had some ability to attract investment and talent. I wavered on whether I should score this as a 2 or a 3. In many cases, we were able to bring in some fantastic new team members who had just the right experience in the areas we wanted to enhance in the plan. The draw of working on an iconic brand that helps learners around the world certainly helped.

Did I have the capital I needed to accelerate the business? Technically, no. We were a small-cap ed-tech business that had been in turnaround mode for quite a while. We also spent much of our cash to help fuel Lexia, which was the appropriate decision, but it didn't leave us with many options for reinvestment. For instance, we had to pull back on much of our larger initiatives, like reinvestment in our brand. So the score could have been a 16 if I were to score this with a 2. I opted to leave it at a 3, which adds up to a solid 24. *Score: 3.*

Insight Score: 24.

GameHouse's Insight Score

I joined RealNetworks in August of 2019. Well, I actually rejoined the business, because I had worked there in the high-flying Web 1.0 days of the Internet in the late nineties. The company had a lot of challenges, including a tumultuous relationship between the CEO and the board. That is a bit of Shakespearian tragedy that we do not need to explore now.

We had a games business that had been an early pioneer in casual gaming on PCs. The company had invented the category but had since been marginalized by leaders in that space. Our marching orders changed significantly based on the operating structure, from "grow the business" to "sell the business" and then back to "grow the business." Let's break down the Insight Score.

TAM: Gaming as a category had and still has a huge TAM. PC gaming was shrinking, and the social and mobile gaming categories were still very large. Even still, Big Fish Games had a large and growing PC games business. *Score: 3.*

Timing: RealNetworks was late to the party. We had a mobile gaming hit called *Doodle Jump*. We hadn't developed it, but we did have a hit that contributed tens of millions of dollars to the business. Social gaming was taking off; we even bought a small gaming studio in Vancouver, Canada. Social casino was also taking off, with other companies already having found most of the high-value customers. And there were successful pivots from our space underway from companies like King, who were heavily pivoting to social and mobile games (pre-*Candy Crush*). In short, we were late coming into the business and had a lot of different strategies. *Score: 1.*

Track Record: RealNetworks had a strong track record in gaming. Heck, it largely invented casual PC gaming with a product called RealArcade. That success of building a product as a one-time experience is very different than building a living, breathing game as a service, which is what many games are like now. RealNetworks didn't have that experience. As previously mentioned, we tried to buy it—but we never did crack the code. *Score 2.*

Plan: There certainly wasn't a cohesive plan when I started. We were in the midst of a platform merge between two gaming sites. They tried to do social games and mobile games, create new downloadable PC games, and, heck, even had a core game service business that companies like GameStop ran on top of. Let's just say the plan wasn't cohesive. And admittedly, my plan wasn't much better. I tried to get into social casino games without much success. *Score: 1.*

Momentum: We were a small-cap public company that was trading at its book value, which basically means that investors thought it was worth as much as its cash—in other words, it had no future value. We couldn't retain and attract the top-notch talent required to really make a pivot into the new form of gaming the way King was doing. We also couldn't make bold bets with our capital because we had several other businesses using our cash, and we didn't have enough currency in our stock to fund large acquisitions. We did make a couple of tuck-in acquisitions (otherwise known as small acquisitions). These can work really well when you have an existing "going and growing" business model to plop that business onto, but they don't work as well when you don't have a platform. *Score: 2.*

Insight Score: 14. Not a great score. Hindsight is twenty-twenty, but clearly, I should have assessed this opportunity with more scrutiny. The marching orders were that we were going to take the company private. But you should be wary of taking on a business where the promise of financial return overshadows your interest in the business or your ability to make it successful.

Interpreting Your Score

If your "TAM" and "timing" totals are low and your score is under 24, then you'd better pivot. If you can control the momentum component because you're doing something as a leader, or if an operator is sabotaging your business, then you can fix that. The easier components to solve are "track record" and "plan," because they are typically in your control—unlike the macro environment.

Here are some overall thoughts on how to approach a low score, organized by variable.

Interpreting Your Score

Variable	Explanation	Action
TAM is a low score.	If your total addressable market is too small, then you should really think about pivoting—or waiting, if you are convinced the market will evolve. If you have enough time, maybe a large enough TAM will materialize. Virtual reality is like that—it hasn't happened yet, but maybe it will. I have a friend named Chia Chin Lee who started a VR gaming company called BigBox VR. He plugged away at it for years when others had abandoned the effort, then sold his business to Facebook for a large sum in 2021, five or six years after everyone had declared virtual reality gaming dead. He had raised enough money to wait.	Pivot or wait.
Timing is wrong.	Timing is tricky, as I mentioned earlier. Use some of those data-based bread crumbs discussed in Part Two. These are early signals that the market is ready and has early consumer interest. If you are not getting those signs, then look to pivot into something else.	Pivot or wait.
Track record is horrible.	If your business hasn't performed well in the past, but you believe there's great ability to accelerate it, then forget the past. Raise the capital and reinvest in the team. Be quantitative regarding this decision. Options here include private equity if it's an old asset that needs to be turned around, taken private, or restructured, etc.	Raise capital if TAM and timing are high.

Plan is bad.	This is probably the easiest component to change because it's in your control. Reach out to consultants and your network, hire a better team, etc. This is on you. As the operator, you should strategically be guiding the team. If you can't, then you need to fire yourself and hire your replacement. If the other scores are higher, then you're responsible.	Easy to fix.
Momentum ain't happening.	If momentum is the biggest issue, work out why. If it's hiring a good team, is the issue that you can't find the talent, or is it your hiring practices, or is it that you can't afford them? If you can't raise capital, is it because you're not an investable business leader or entrepreneur? Generally, if the first four variables of the Insight Score are strong and you can't get capital or talent, then there's something about you that's the issue. If your overall score is lower, then of course you won't be able to find the best talent or raise capital. It's rare that the first variables of the Insight Score are high and yet you cannot raise capital or get funding for a project.	Impossible to fix if the preceding score is low. Should be easy if the preceding score is high.

I'm not trying to be prescriptive for every business, because every business is unique. But as you walk through the scoring, issues will surface. Work through those findings and observations with your team, your mentors, and industry experts. Collaboration and transparency are vital to ensure that you don't waste time and capital.

The Ability to Act

Hopefully this book was able to contribute to your analysis of your business. The Insight Score can be a helpful guide for evaluating whether you can change or enhance your market position. As I mentioned in the beginning, I am not of the mind that you have to throw in the proverbial towel if you are not already a market leader. There are many paths to the top. Every business is different, and only you and your team, after careful study, will have the best view on the path forward. Please do not immediately take an investor's or a board member's advice on hiring an expensive consulting firm. This outsourcing of your business IQ only masks the heavy lifting of your own strategic planning process—and your accountability to the plan. It's always easy to say that it was "the consultants' plan."

The reason momentum is such an important factor in the Insight Score comes down to the willingness to act. I am reminded of a scene in Christopher Nolan's 2005 movie *Batman Begins*, in which Henri Ducard/Ra's al Ghul tells his young protégé, Bruce Wayne, "Training is nothing! The will is everything. The will to act."

If you have the willingness to act, you can accomplish amazing things. Momentum is really the "ability to act." It enables you to chart a course forward. To charge the hill. To mount a push toward your biggest, hairiest, most audacious goals. At the end of the day as a leader, your true power is to make sure that you don't run out of money in your business and that you can acquire more capital to grow it.

I would encourage you to take on the task of your business's self-actualization. Drive a planning process using the work in this book, and hopefully I will hear all about your amazing success. And remember to enjoy the journey. You only have one life, and work comprises such a large part of what gives us value and meaning. Don't squander your time on a venture that doesn't feed you.

Your job as CEO/founder is to make the organizational objectives and goals for your business clear, concise, and measurable. I am reminded of Jack Palance's character as the wise and crusty old cowboy in the movie *City Slickers*, who tells Billy Crystal's character to figure out what his "one thing" is in his life. In business, you need to wrap all of the complexities in all of the specific strategies and tactics around something simple that everyone can understand and strive for. I've worked for companies that had so many initiatives and goals, it was hard to get a cohesive picture of what everyone was actually trying to do. Decide what your "one thing" is for your business.

You might have guessed that I am a huge superhero aficionado. As a kid, I loved how Stan Lee, the founder of Marvel Comics, would sign off each comic book to his readers with an enthusiastic, "Excelsior!" It's a Latin word for "ever upward." Well, true believers, you pioneers, you stewards of potential...

Excelsior!

ACKNOWLEDGMENTS

OFTEN DESCRIBE MYSELF as being totally amiable to most people—as long as they "do not tell me what to do." At the end of the day, we have to live our lives the way we see fit, the way we want to live them. My high school graduation yearbook quoted one of my favorites, Groucho Marx. I love his saying, "I refuse to join any club that would have me as a member." As soon as things get comfortable or familiar, I just like to stir the pot. If you have ever seen the 2006 comedic film *Talladega Nights*, the antagonist father (Reese Bobby) would often get kicked out of the restaurant Applebee's when the family situation was getting a bit comfortable and serene. I love the line (before he caused a ruckus and was summarily kicked out of the restaurant), "Yep, I guess things are just about perfect... it's making me feel kind of itchy." So thank you for putting up with me, whether you like me or don't like me.

This book is a love letter to every business leader, entrepreneur, and dreamer that needed a bit of guidance or mentorship on how to fix or grow their business. I was lucky to have been privileged in my own life by the many people who shaped the man I am today. From a professional perspective, the folks who were key to my career development and helped me develop my operating view of the world include: Pat Tyson, Jill Levine, Kevin Klustner, Evan Kaplan, Rob Glaser, Maria Cantwell, Bruce Jacobsen, Mika Salmi, Mike Moritz, Heather Redman, Michael Comish, Rich Barton, Erik Blachford, Byron Bishop, Stu Robertson, Mitch Robinson, Simon Tam, Patti Elliot, Holly Nordal, Barry Diller, Rich Tong, Michelle Goldberg, Dave Cotter, Greg Harrison, Bill Bryant, John Barbour, Wilf Russell, Brad Wiskirchen, Glenn Michael, Alex Moore, Melanie Knueven, Chris McClave, David Niu, Dave Hajdu, Ben Gilbert, Geoff Entress, Mike Galgon, John Hass, Nick Gaehde, the Rosetta Stone board of directors, and the entire Rosetta Stone team. Finally, a special acknowledgment to my team members who have passed, Angie Weber and Patrick Lofy. I think about them every day.

I have worked for some fantastically intelligent leaders who taught me everything I know about scaling and turning around businesses. I've also worked for some real assholes— all of them famous in the world of business—who have taught me completely different lessons. With proper perspective, I have to thank them too.

As I was writing this book, so many people provided me with inspiration, help, and support. I would like to spotlight a couple of those wonderful individuals. First, I would like to thank Andrea Riggs for the encouragement and the countless hours she spent copywriting the original manuscript before I sent it to the publisher. She was a pillar for me when I ran into self-doubt. Second, I have to thank Jason Kuder, who helped me systemize all of my slides, notes, and thoughts. He helped develop the Insight Score with me too. He helped to turn a stale concept into a more cogent and holistic set of doctrines. Lastly, I would like to thank Page Two, my publisher. The entire team has been fantastic, and there are so many members I would like to thank—in particular, Trena White, Scott Steedman, and Adrineh Der-Boghossian. They made my job easier and the book so much better. I am also so thankful for the business leaders who I cajoled into contributing to this work: Niklas Hed, Rob Solomon, Riccardo Zacconi, Laurence Franklin, Judy Goldberg, Nick Gaehde, Soumeya Benghanem, Mike Hilton, and Peter Denton.

I would like to acknowledge my family and friends, including my biological and non-biological parents. Frankly, there's so much family to list that I will run the risk of inadvertently forgetting someone. I dedicated this book to my mom because she sacrificed so much for my brother and me. She deserves the credit, since she taught us many valuable lessons and raised us to be the people we are today. I wish she had born into a different time and circumstances, because she would have been a fantastic entrepreneur. My wonderful immediate family means the world to me. My children— Chloe, Jack, and Pete—are my greatest prizes. My wife, Anne, is the sweetest, most empathic, most determined person I have ever met. She patiently endured my long working hours and overall obsession with this book. I receive an incredible amount of inspiration watching her creative and entrepreneurial endeavors. In particular, it has been very inspiring to watch my wife grow her business, Rock Grace. She turned this idea—that the world needs a better alternative to alcohol— into a thriving business, all by herself. She used many of the principles in this book and many new ones from her own incredible intuition.

Finally, to all my friends, colleagues, teammates, connections, and family members, I thank you for your love and friendship.

I'd like to encourage anyone who has read this book but who felt like they couldn't achieve whatever they wanted to do to leave it with a feeling that you *can* achieve your goals. You're never too old or too young to build something amazing. If I look back at some of the roles I've taken, I probably would not have taken them if I had truly understood how daunting they would be. Ignorance can sometimes be bliss. Simply live your life (personal or professional) in the manner that you want to live it. Be smart, be strategic, and think through whether you have the right idea or business to make an incredible impact on the world. Don't listen to the naysayers, if you believe you have a vision and a plan for success.

I believe we live in an incredible time. I am more optimistic about the future than ever. There are large, difficult, and sometimes scary problems that we need to resolve. But I am very confident that, with the right financial and environmental conditions, the human spirit will rally for a better future.

INDEX

Note: Page references in italics refer to figures

ability to act, 229–31
AdXpose, 9, 30–31
Andreessen, Marc, 5, 99–100
Apple: as aggregator, 84, 95; app ecosystem, 65, 66, 95; Epic Games lawsuit, 85, 92, 96; financial efficiency, 175
AtomFilms, 6–7, 44

B2B, 21, 24–31, 31–36, 59, 103–5, 134
Benghanem, Soumeya (interview), 118–20
Boston Consulting Group, 3–4
brands: alignment, 30, 39, 186; awareness, 34, 36–37, 49, 54, 90, 224, 225; creation, 69, 72, 102; cross-selling, 136; customer retention, 127–28; growth, 86; partnerships, 53–54, 132–37, 138; timing, 51; uniqueness, 38, 96, 107–8
business-to-business (B2B). *See* B2B

case studies: B2B segments, 103–5; Expedia, 31–36, 87–91; Mpire, 22–23, 24–31; RealNetworks, 114–17; Rosetta Stone, 36–39, 107–8; WRQ, 92–94
Coach, 134
Collins, Jim, 154, 155
communicate the plan: BHAG (Big Hairy Audacious Goals), 154–58; communication framework, 158–60; continual communication, 160–62; corporate culture, promoting, 153–54; employee satisfaction, 165–66; Insight Score, 168; mission statement, 157; reinforce message, 163–64; takeaways, 166–67; vision statement, 154–55
competitive advantage: competition, 213; Expedia, 90–91; Microsoft, 93–94, 115–17; relative advantage, 36, 107, 111, 117, 121, 182; strategy, 37–38, *38*; TAM, 20
competitive value analysis: case study, RealNetworks, 114–17;

ABOUT
THE AUTHOR

MATT HULETT has driven more than $2 billion in value creation as a four-time public company CEO and president and a two-time private company CEO. He is a seasoned technology executive with more than thirty years of experience building and leading world-class SaaS and consumer companies. He has had multiple turnaround successes in the public and private sectors, including Rosetta Stone, RealNetworks, and Expedia. He is regularly featured in technology and business podcasts and media outlets, such as *Recode*, *Forbes*, and *Entrepreneur*. Matt lives in Seattle with his wife, Anne (CEO of Rock Grace), and their three children.

You've read the book. Now it's time to unlock your company.

This book is my love letter to the 99 percent of businesses that are not market leaders. It is all about taking business leaders through a journey across five steps that will help them determine whether they can unlock value for their company. If you have gotten this far in the book to be reading this page, I hope it has helped you to "unlock" your business.

Don't stop now—keep the momentum going in three steps!

1. Write an Amazon review and receive free stuff.
If you did receive value from the book, I would greatly appreciate it if you could write a positive review on Amazon. I will return your generosity by sending you my own personal *Unlock* planning templates. After you write the review, just email me at matthulett@gmail.com and I will send them to you directly!

2. Buy *Unlock* for your teams.
Unlock is a great resource as the basis to your regular business planning. Please email me at matthulett@gmail.com for special discounts on bulk orders. I will include my own proprietary planning templates with all bulk orders.

3. Check out my website.
If you are interested in diving deeper into my work, then please check out my website: startupwhisperer.com. Subscribe to my mailing list and you will get access to free content, including the online *Unlock* assessment.

Onward and upwards!

matthulett@gmail.com

⊕ **startupwhisperer.com**

🐦 **matt_hulett**

in **matthulett**